CLEAR ROUND!

CLEAR ROUND!

Interviews by Julia Longland

Mayflower Books/Barrie & Jenkins
Mayflower Books, Inc.
New York 10022

Created by The Wordsmiths Company Limited

Published by Barrie & Jenkins Limited
24 Highbury Crescent
London N5 1RX

Published in the United States by Mayflower Books, Inc.,
New York, N.Y. 10022
Originally published in England by Barrie & Jenkins Limited,
London

ISBN 0–8317–0012–2

The creators and publishers acknowledge:

Julia Longland and Ann Martin (interviews and authorship)
Findlay Davidson (research and photographs)
Budd of New York (photograph page 75)
Kay Williams (editing)
Ann Warne (sketches)
and the champions and their colleagues, who made the book
possible.

Manufactured in Great Britain

First American Edition

Contents

Foreword

Douglas Bunn

former international rider, proprietor of All England Show Jumping Course at Hickstead, and member of international judges' panel

I hope readers get as much pleasure reading this book as I have from reading the manuscript. My first reaction on being asked to write this Foreword was, frankly – yet *another* book on showjumping and eventing which would add very little to what most of us know already.

How wrong I was!

It is a scholarly work, and very well researched. The opening and closing chapters are good archivistic material. I know most of the riders featured very well but I was fascinated and entertained to read so much about them which was completely new to me. Furthermore, it is all done with a lightness of style that takes the reader galloping through the pages. Julia Longland has in her portraits truly captured the character of the different riders and their own comments are invariably most illuminating!

Miss Longland did ask me to write something about my own riding. I had a funny sort of riding career in that I had also to fit in my practice at the Bar, create and foster Hickstead, as well as build up a large business – all of which, as I tried to explain to the author, is very boring compared to David Broome winning the World Championship on Beethoven! However, I would not have missed it for anything.

I suppose the highlight of my jumping career was in 1939! When I was eleven I rode four ponies in a hotly contested Junior Championship at the Royal Counties Show and finished first, second, third and fourth after about four or five jumps-off. I am proud of the fact that I was nearly always considered good enough to represent my country in the 'first' team. To win a Nations Cup is always an exhilarating experience; the Daily Express Foxhunter Final is a nice one to win. I am sure other riders felt the same way but I always thought that I was champion at coming second! Twice in the Rome Grand Prix, the King's Cup and others too numerous to mention!

Hickstead came into being so that a lot of people could have a lot of fun. I always remind myself (and others) of this when the going gets tough. I would not pretend that I do not get great satisfaction from seeing what it has done for horses and riders.

Some years ago a nice old boy used to appear at Hickstead from time to time to watch the contests. He used to wear patent leather shoes, sponge bag trousers, a boater, and used to sport a magnificent moustache. He also carried an impressive looking black bag in which he carried his luncheon. When we first ran a European Championship here, I pointed out this gentleman to Mrs. Carruthers (the course-builder) and explained to her that he was the Technical Delegate from the FEI. He disappeared into the men's toilet before she quite reached him. However, she was patient and when he reappeared she greeted him in French, ushered him round all the fences and expressed the hope that he was satisfied with everything. This retired gentleman from Brighton was most impressed with his reception and said everything was admirable! When Pamela later met the real Technical Delegate I had to go into hiding for an hour or two. I think this little incident gave me as much pleasure as the hundreds of fun things that have happened at Hickstead over the years.

This is a book I can guarantee you will refer to time and time again.

Miss Julia Longland is to be congratulated.

Preface

Julia Longland

It is impossible to consider skill in equestrian sport without thinking of the expertise of David Broome, who has taken away the breath of many millions of spectators in his pursuit of victory, and yet another 'clear round!'

Over the years, world championships, European titles, Olympic medals, show championships, grand prix have been won and lost. And always the compulsive question from the spectator's seat: how will Broome employ his skill this time? Will he treat his rivals as he did on the last occasion? Or will he try something new?

For me his most dramatic performance took place at Hickstead, in the final of the 1969 Men's European Showjumping Championship. Broome was lying equal 2nd with the great German veteran Hans Günther Winkler, and both men were one point behind Alwin Schockemöhle; significantly, Broome was in his favourite challenging position – just behind the leader.

There were really only two of them concerned with the death – Broome and Schockemöhle, who had battled all the way round Europe and across to the Mexico Olympics in the previous nine years. Even their horses were superstars: the Irish-bred chestnut, Mister Softee, versus the hugely-muscled Hanoverian, Donald Rex. Winkler, the most powerful of champions on his day, had a lesser contender in Enigk and was playing a supporting role.

So the stage was set. The final course was jumped over 18 fences in the first round: six speed, six puissance and six Nations Cup fences. The competitors went in reverse order to their placings, and when his turn came, Broome set Mister Softee alight. Not forgetting that a speed aggregate of the two rounds would be decisive in the event of equality of faults, Broome made everyone clutch the palms of their hands as he sent Softee on at a hair-raising pace.

Like the champion he was, Softee responded and gave Britain the first clear round. Winkler and Enigk, disliking the hot pace, became ruffled and hit the first part of the treble. Schockemöhle, however, stood up to the pressure and was clear with Donald Rex, but exposed an Achilles' heel – his time was three seconds slower.

David Broome now scented victory, and moved in for the kill. In the second round, with the puissance fences removed, he drove Softee on to gallop even faster. The four white stockings flashed in the sunlight, hooves skimming each fence with never an inch to spare. It was too mad a pace, some thought, as the pair cut in to the double of gates and flew down the treble. But the magic held and they finished without an error in an extremely fast time.

Broome was aware of two facts at this moment: one, that Softee, who could win a speed class as well as a puissance with equal expertise, was an economical jumper, able to adapt to a long or short stride without breaking his rhythm and concentration; and, two, that though Donald Rex could jump fast, he could get rattled if asked to treat the big obstacles in the abandoned manner of a Gamblers' Stakes.

Though Schockemöhle picked up the challenge with ferocious courage, he must have known he was in a tactical trap, for he had to finish in under 62 seconds to win. Over the first few fences, Donald Rex let rip with a flat-out gallop, but doom was in sight as Schockemöhle turned him in for a desperate effort at the final treble. Unbalanced, they hit the first two elements and it was all quickly over.

So a master tactician won the day, and wrote equestrian history by securing his third European title, on a horse who was also achieving his third European title (though once with a different rider). Commented David Broome: 'Softee was poetry in motion'; and so he was.

But that was only one great moment of many. For the selection in this book, the great horsemen and women of the world have singled out the moments of their career *they* remember as the best – either in victory or in defeat. It is their deeds which have brought honour to equestrian sport in the years past; and it is their own words which now bring those deeds to life.

—Julia Longland   England 1978

The Making of the Stars

From the moment he first allowed man to clamber onto his back, the horse was to play a vital role in the shaping of the world's history. Once tamed, he endowed man with the magical power of mobility, enabling him to travel overland and establish the roots of civilization. As chariot-puller and, later, as cavalry mount, the horse became an essential weapon of war. In times of peace, he became a creature of majesty for exhibition, an instrument of enjoyment in leisure riding; and throughout the centuries he has been a willing participant in feats of sport, daring and endurance.

All kinds of record survive from antiquity to chronicle the horse's progress through the ages. Solomon is believed to have kept a high-class stable, which included horses imported from Asia Minor and Egypt; and riding was known in Babylon during Nebuchadnezzar's reign, c. 1200 BC. Horsemanship is known to have been greatly revered by the Ancient Greeks: Alexander the Great (reigned 336–323 BC) owed much of his military success to the cavalry originated by his father, Philip II of Macedon, who in turn owed much to the philosopher and historian Xenophon, a master of horse whose remarkable treaty on equitation, *Hippike*, is still consulted today.

In Ancient Rome, too, the expert horseman was highly regarded. In the public games, riders swooped from barebacked steeds at full gallop to pick up objects from the ground; and *desultores* ('circus-riders') leapt from one horse to another at speed. Pliny the Elder tells us that the favourite in a race wore a popular colour to enable the crowd to distinguish him from the other riders. Wealthy Romans who rode for leisure, perhaps finding the trot too bone-shaking, began to school their horses in movements that correspond with the piaffer and passage of modern dressage.

The horses ridden by the Greeks and Romans were probably naturalized descendants of the Bactrian horse from Central Asia, and therefore light in weight and able to gallop fast and turn neatly. Over the centuries, however, particularly as the use of armour in war began to increase, riders came to depend on the heavier horse; thus schooling, the science of controlling the animal's movements, became ever more important.

Equestrian competition, a tradition in the Middle East, was to appeal to the Crusaders; and jousting tournaments began to be held in England in the 13th century. Originally a team event, the joust came eventually to focus on a severe test of single combat: maintaining his seat against the shock of impact, the knight had to keep his own lance accurately aimed while driving his horse straight ahead at full gallop. At Smithfield Horse Sales, near what is now the City of London, 13th-century prospective buyers could judge a horse's capacity for speed by witnessing impromptu races; though history does not record whether the lightweight boy jockeys rode straight-legged with feet well forward, like the knight, or crouched forward, like the modern rider.

It was not until the 17th century, however, when farming land began to be divided into fields, that jumping became important in England. The hedges and ditches that formed the new boundaries became obstacles to be cleared by the rider, and following hounds across country soon came to be regarded as a daring pursuit. Further efforts by the farmer to contain his stock naturally resulted in greater obstacles for the horseman: for example, the post-and-rails fence, designed to prevent cattle from getting stuck in ditches; from the timber rails, original hedge and probably a ditch on the far side protected by another post-and-rails, evolved the 'double

oxer'. Post-and-rails, barred stiles, high palings, stone walls, single and double banks: original solid fences such as these have survived only in Ireland; elsewhere, they are rarely seen today outside the show ring. The word 17th-century riders used for the new sport of clearing obstacles was not 'jumping' but 'leaping', which continued to describe jumping contests until the late-19th century.

The mounted sports of today differ widely from the ancient equestrian traditions of performance inherited from Asia. As standards of horsemanship became established in Europe and America, achievement came to be seen not only in terms of distance and speed but also in terms of height and lengths jumped. By the beginning of the 20th century, jumping competitions were well established in Britain. In 1876, the Royal Agricultural Hall in Islington had permitted horses to enter 'leaping' events at their show without extra charge; and in 1907, the first (Royal) International Horse Show was held at Olympia under the presidency of the Earl of Lonsdale (whose passion for yellow, echoed in his carriage and furnishings, had earned him the appellation of 'The Yellow Earl').

A class for French showjumpers had been included in a harness horse show in Paris in 1866; 'high leap' and 'wide leap' competitions had been part of the first Royal Dublin Society show, held in 1868; Switzerland held its first jumping competition in Yverdon Racecourse at the turn of the century; and in Germany, the country that was later to produce the most dominant teams in the world, shows (similar to the county shows of England) specializing in horse contests became very popular. At the 1900 Olympic Games in Paris, Van

'Col. Mike': Sir Mike Ansell, the architect of British showjumping's development after the Second World War.

Vangendonck of Belgium took the gold medal with a long jump of 20 ft 0 in; the high-jump gold went to Gardère of France, who cleared 6 ft 0 in.

North America was to prove as enthusiastic as Europe about the new sport of showjumping. The National Horse Show, first held at Madison Square Garden in 1883, is still the grand social occasion of the Fall season; rich owners, then as now, kept a string of horses for professionals to jump. In Canada, as in many other countries, army officers played a major part in the early international jumping teams. In 1909, a team of Canadian officers visited Olympia, London, where Capt. W. T. Evans on Confidence cleared 7 ft to take the high-jump competition. (Canada held at that time the world record: professional Hugh Wilson on Pearl had jumped 7 ft 6¾ in at Des Moines, Iowa, in 1902.) After World War I, Canada started her own international show with the Royal Agricultural Winter Fair at Toronto, in 1922; today, the Fair is the traditional end to the North American Fall circuit, which starts at Harrisburg, runs on to Washington and New York, and closes the season for a number of European and most American riders.

Back in Britain, civilian and military riders dedicated to showjumping met to attempt to stabilize the peculiar rules – which allowed marks for style as well as faults for knockdowns to be given – governing the sport. Lord Lonsdale agreed to become president and Col. V. D. S. Williams secretary of the British Show Jumping Association, formed in 1923 with the aim of improving standards of judging. Equestrian sport had already been granted international recognition, with the foundation in 1921 of the Fédération Equestre Internationale (FEI); and thus, at the 1924 Paris Olympics, the three-day event, showjumping and dressage had been run under standardized rules.

Col. Mike Ansell, a figure who was to dominate British showjumping after the war, first appeared in international events in the late 1920s. He won at Olympia on Mousie in 1930, and in the next year, when a captain in the Royal Inniskillings, competed in New York in the British Army team, which also included the late Jack Talbot-Ponsonby, the famous post-war course-builder. Lt. Talbot-Ponsonby was to achieve the magic treble of three King George V Gold Cups; but it was Ansell whose visionary genius was to transform show-jumping from just another sport into star-studded entertainment.

The growth of equestrian sport in Germany between World Wars I and II was heavily underscored by the 1936 Olympic Games in Berlin, where a massive crowd of some 120,000 in the main stadium saw their home team win the showjumping gold medal. Germany took the three-day-event and dressage gold medals, too, while Britain achieved the distinction of her first-ever equestrian medal: the three-day-event team bronze.

In America, too, important developments were afoot. In 1937, the American Horse Shows Association (AHSA) took control of the US Cavalry Association's membership of the FEI, thus causing the army to cede its power in the sport to the civilian. Another step was the establishing of five separate zones across the United States (there are now 11), to ensure balanced development of the sport in such a vast area.

The outbreak of World War II brought equestrian sport to a standstill, and many of the horses were commandeered. But 1939 had seen the further emergence of two brilliant men: Mike Ansell, who rode in international teams

on the Continent and saw – for the last time in his life – the excitement potential of the sport at first-hand; and Mickey Brinckmann, who won the Grand Prix at Aachen and led his team to an astonishing Nations Cup victory over the Rumanians – 9 faults to 87. Brinckmann, who became famous as the course-builder at Aachen and regular coach to the German Olympic team, was to be the architect of the showjumping courses at the 1972 Munich Olympics.

Mike Ansell, commanding the 1st Lothian & Border Yeomanry, suffered a tragic accident early in the war. Trapped in a loft with some of his men at St. Valéry, France, in 1940, he was caught in a crossfire of British bullets and all but blinded. He was captured and spent a long time in prisoner-of-war camps, going at intervals to Paris for eye operations. With 'Colonel Mike' in Oflag IXAH at Spanenburg, Germany, were two other showjumping men: Major Nat Kindersley and Major Bede Cameron. Together the three men talked horses, gave lectures and dreamt up an outdoor international horse show that was to revolutionize the post-war sport. Repatriated in 1944, Colonel Mike became Chairman and Vice-President of the BSJA; and on September 1st 1945, he launched the first International Show to be held at the White City.

From the start, Colonel Mike, aware of the potentially vast audiences, aimed to attract not only the traditionally horsey people but also local Londoners who wanted a day out. He had a tremendous flair for publicity, for showmanship, for timing – and his sense of colour was remarkable in a man who could not see. When, 25 years later, he was asked to move the show out of London to Hickstead

A legendary pairing in action at the Royal International Horse Show in July 1960, then held at the White City, London: Wilf White and Nizefela.

because both the the White City and Wembley Stadium venues had become 'impossible', Colonel Mike refused. His admirable reason: 'My barber, a Londoner who likes to have an evening out at the horse show, wouldn't be able to go.'

The Ansell formula flourished. In 1946, there were two horse shows in the White City stadium; the second, the September Victory Championship, was won by the man whose name was to become a household word: Colonel Harry Llewellyn. Llewellyn, already an established amateur steeplechase rider who had finished 2nd and 4th in the Grand National, and a showjumper as well, was nevertheless given fierce competition in the jump-off by one Douglas Bunn, aged 18, who finished as runner-up.

By the next year, 1947, the stage was set for the début of Foxhunter, the horse who was to become a superstar in the Hollywood tradition, receiving sacks of fanmail every week at his home near Abergavenny, in Monmouthshire. Foxhunter's arrival coincided with Colonel Mike's determination to bring equestrian sport to the populace as a whole, whether in written, spoken or televised form; it was Ansell's inspiration that prompted the first showjumping programme on television, presented from the 1947 Royal International Horse Show at the White City, by Peter Dimmock.

Thus did the magic names of the 1950s become familiar faces: Pat Smythe on Tosca and Prince Hal, Wilf White on Nizefela, Alan Oliver on Red Admiral, Peter Robeson on Craven A, Brian Butler on Tankard and, of course, Harry Llewellyn on Foxhunter. Foxhunter, who won the King George V Gold Cup three times, an Olympic team bronze and

'One Douglas Bunn' ... is here riding Sun Valley at the 1969 Horse of the Year Show.

an Olympic team gold and countless other trophies, became a symbol of patriotism to a nation of horse-lovers. Sunday Express sportswriter Alan Hoby even travelled up to Abergavenny to interview the famous equine star.

Today, television-viewing figures in Britain are higher for equestrian events (10,000,000 a night for the major shows) than for any other sport, except soccer. Many factors have contributed to this boom – indeed, it can be seen almost as a series of charges exploding along a fuse wire. Sponsors and escalating prize-money have followed in the wake of the media exposure of showjumping and eventing: £20,000 for equestrian prize money in 1954 had become nearly £750,000 ($1,500,000) by 1977. The extension of the indoor jumping season throughout the winter means that events are going on all the year round, and therefore demands double the number of horses. Commuter travel has given professional riders increased mobility; though many British professionals prefer to stick to the old-fashioned horsebox method of transport.

In America, growth of television coverage, and therefore of sponsorship, of equestrian events has been much slower, chiefly owing to the vast distance that separates viewers from the event. Until very recently, it was hard work for former Olympic champion Billy Steinkraus to persuade an American network to accept showjumping in a package deal for coast-to-coast viewing. Much progress has been made on regional programmes, however, and the number of showjumping grand prix is now two or three times greater than it was 10 years ago. Eventing, too, lacking the magic aura of Britain's star patron, the Duke of Beaufort, who started Badminton in 1949 and gave cross-country riding to the man in the street, was very slow to capture the American imagination; though, happily, the team and individual gold medals from Montreal have made quite an impact.

One factor in establishing the popularity of showjumping on British television may have been the ingenious placing of the cameras round the arena, to give a close-up of the rider's face, or of the horse's eye. Close-ups give an immediate intimacy, an urgency, an ability to share joy and suffering; and the viewer's resulting sense of involvement has helped to turn Harvey Smith and David Broome into stars. But many people have contributed to the growing popularity of the horse. One of the earliest radio broadcasters on showjumping at a time when few people had television sets, was commentator Brian Johnston. His first programme covered the 1948 King George V Gold Cup at the White City, just after the Olympic Games in Wembley Stadium, where the British team had won a bronze medal. Thirty years on, Brian still vividly recalls his words: 'And it's Foxhunter, coming clear over the last. ...'

That spark of urgency and excitement set alight a new generation of horsemen: the showjumping superstars.

Richard Meade

Born on December 4th 1938, Richard Meade is the only son of John and Phyllis O'Mahoney Meade, who run a Connemara Pony Stud near Chepstow, South Wales. From an early age, Richard absorbed the traditions of hunting and the Pony Club: his parents were, for some years, joint-masters of the Curre Foxhounds, who hunt the steep, wooded hill country at the southern end of the Wye valley.

In 1954 he first tasted serious competition, as a member of the Monmouth Pony Club team that won the Area Championship at Glenusk. He rode the 17-hh Grade C jumper St. Teilo, which was loaned by a neighbour who was to prove a constant source of encouragement over the years – Col. Harry Llewellyn. In the final at Tetbury, Richard and St. Teilo won the Boys' Championship and helped the team to finish 2nd. And that moment the ambition to go three-day eventing was born.

At Lancing College Richard played Eton Fives, represented the school in athletics, excelled at mathematics and formed a love of music and photography – interests that were to remain in the years to come. Before going up to Magdalene College, Cambridge (where he read engineering), Richard completed National Service in the 11th Hussars. In 1962, Richard teamed up with Miss

C. C. Clements' Barberry, a seven-year-old thoroughbred from a line of horses bred by the Clements family at their Kildare stud for over 150 years. With Barberry, Richard joined a British team for an international students' rally in Amsterdam that summer, and a year later was selected for what was to be the top team at the three-day-event championship in Munich.

At the Tokyo Olympics in 1964, Barberry led after cross-country day, but then dropped back to 8th place. Richard was thereafter a regular member of the British team for the next four years, and rode Miss Mary Gordon-Watson's Cornishman to a team gold medal at the Mexico Olympics after Barberry injured his back at Burghley, a month before the Games.

In 1970 and 1971 he rode Capt. Martin Whiteley's The Poacher; when, in 1972, The Poacher was retired, Richard scored Olympic victories on Maj. Derek Allhusen's Laurieston. In 1973, he rode Mrs. Ba Hammond's Eagle Rock – coincidentally, bred by Mr. and Mrs. Meade – at Badminton. Successes with Mrs. Henry Wilkin's bay Wayfarer, with Jacob Jones and with Mr. Michael Abraham's Tommy Buck kept Richard in the results sheet. He married in 1977, and is an insurance consultant.

'And so there I was, soaked to the skin, peering through a blanket of torrential rain, about to tackle the cross-country course of an Olympic Games, and I really wondered whether a horse could see the fences with the water bashing against his eyeballs.' A comment by Richard Meade on the start of one of his most extraordinary and rewarding experiences as an international horseman: the victory of the British three-day-event team at the 1968 Mexico Olympics.

'The most exciting thing was Mexico. Munich was tremendous, of course – exciting in retrospect, I think – but Mexico was a breakthrough. For the first time since Stockholm in 1956, Britain had got back into a winning position at the Olympics, and we all felt we had achieved something special. It was a very happy team, and a very happy place to be in. The Mexicans are sunny, fun-loving people, and I think we caught the atmosphere right from the beginning.

'Then there was the terrible adversity of the conditions, the most enormous challenge. It was a most colourful and dramatic experience riding in those Games – the contrast between wonderful sunshine and torrential rain, and the transformation of the cross-country course into the toughest test of endurance any of us had ever seen. Mexico was a fairy-tale setting.

'I remember the Chef d'Equipe, Colonel Bill Lithgow, literally soaked to the skin in his shirt sleeves as I started on the cross-country with Cornishman.' The timekeeper, also dripping wet, started the countdown – normally a very serious moment, the rider's thoughts racing over the dangers ahead as he winds up to spring away to a good start. 'You could only see 20 yards in front of you, with the steam and the intense rain. Nobody in Europe realized just what it was like. It was almost laughable to think that this was the

Olympic Games, the culmination of four years' effort and training.' Richard was 34th of the 48 starters to go, and third in the team. But by the time it was his turn, what had started as an ordinary cross-country course had, after $4^{1}/_{2}$ inches of rain in 90 minutes, become a nightmare of flooded rivers.

'I had a peaked cap on, which was at least some protection against the deluge, but Cornishman had nothing, and it seemed impossible to me that he could really see through the rain to judge what he was going to jump. Visibility was down to 10 or 15 yards, and I did not even have the advantage of knowing him well, as we had become acquainted just before the Games and had only jumped two or three cross-country fences together in training. So we were strangers thrown together in some crazy adventure, each trusting completely in the other because we had no option.'

The craziness of Avandaro, the mountain village outside Mexico City where the Olympic three-day event was staged, happened when a freak storm swept down from the mountains to drench the golf course and plateau of the competition site. It was something quite apart from the daily rain shower, which the riders had come to expect as normal and which did nothing to damage the course.

Two horses from each country had already been round the cross-country, and even without the storm, which only got under way as the second horses started, a Russian horse had fallen at the 22nd fence and broken her neck; though some reports had said she could not get up from the water and drowned. And by the time Richard went, one rider who could not swim had nearly drowned in a rain-swollen river. The Russians had also created a diversion by trying to make use of walkie-talkies attached to observers from their team, hidden in the bushes of the steeplechase course. These were meant to warn their riders, who carried receiver sets, about conditions prevailing by each jump; but the ruse was discovered.

On the steeplechase course, usually a $2^1/_2$ mile circuit sandwiched between two sections of roads and tracks, where a horse stretches out into a comfortable, rhythmic gallop taking unremarkable 'chase fences in his stride, Cornishman had battled through blinding hail over a set of timber obstacles that bore little resemblance to national hunt racing, to score maximum bonus marks – one of only nine horses to do so that day. This meant he had completed the circuit in exactly the required time.

'By the time the countdown to the start was completed, I had decided that the whole situation was so bizarre it was almost funny. How could you worry in conditions like these? So Cornishman and I set off. I remember the start of the cross-country course well – the first fence was very brightly painted, a white viaduct footbridge, which Cornishman jumped very well. And almost straightaway he answered one question for me: the second fence, a rail over a ditch, was difficult to identify in the downpour; but he cleared it with ease. I knew now that he could see, and after that we just went on taking everything as it came, and hoping to survive. There was one really bad moment, when Cornishman sank down to his knees in a soggy quagmire of mud over a drop fence, No. 14 – it was just like landing in rice pudding – and I had to sit right back and try to pick him up before we turned a somersault. I gripped as hard as I could with my legs – and I realized what a very, very good horse he was when he somehow struggled back to drag his feet out of the mud and regain his balance, and we went on safely to the finish.

'The last two fences on the course also brought in the river, jumping over it and back again. The last but one, you jumped from a platform, about 3 ft up – the river had risen and the water was sweeping out to the field. They had built up a ledge across the platform to level it horizontally with the ground. By the time the next horse came galloping up, the river had risen so much that it was nearly overflowing its banks, and the water was sweeping over this platform. It was all very dramatic.'

Derek Allhusen and Lochinvar, first to go for Britain, had got round the course without trouble, except for one refusal, then Jane Bullen followed with Our Nobby; and they became victims of the river fence, No. 22. The landing was so holding that Nobby's forelegs sank into the mud and he was unable to pull them out in time. Jane was, in fact, one of the last people to attempt jumping over the river; word travelled back soon afterwards that it was unjumpable and so later horses ploughed through the river crossing instead. Another fall for Nobby at the last fence, when his feet again got stuck in the mud, meant that the last British pair, Ben Jones and The Poacher, had to do fairly well. The rain actually stopped in time for The Poacher, who had to do a lot of swimming with Ben to reach the finish; but they made it, to cheers from the British camp.

Richard and Cornishman eventually finished in 4th place after the final showjumping phase, thus just missing an individual bronze medal. But the team won the gold, and that, for Richard and his colleagues, had been the main object.

'The team competition comes first, and individual honours, whenever they happen to come along, are incidental. If you go all out for

In 1967 the horse was Our Nobby and the rider Jane Bullen at the Palisade fence in the Burghley Horse Trials, just a year before Jane (now Holderness-Roddam) became the first British girl to compete in the Olympic eventing competition, as a team-mate of Richard Meade.

the fastest possible time, you may end up with the gold; but, on the other hand, you may fall flat on your nose and ruin the team's chances. I remember at the Tokyo Olympics, everything was geared to the team, and I was bitterly disappointed when the team was eliminated and only two of us were left to go for individual placings. Then I had a chance of winning the gold with Barberry, when we finished the speed and endurance day in the lead. But disaster struck our showjumping, and we dropped to 8th place.

'Ben Jones had been with me in Japan, and Derek and I had ridden in the team together twice before; Jane was new to the team, but I

had ridden with her elder brother Michael, at Tokyo, and we were all great friends. Her presence – she was the first British woman to ride in an Olympic three-day event – added that extra spark to the team spirit, and when we won at Avandaro the feeling was quite fantastic. The contrast to Tokyo, the triumph we felt at overcoming the horrors, the torrents and the opposition, and this great team achievement were extraordinary.'

The comradeship of that team has become legendary in equestrian history. A nurse from

The then Lt. Mark Phillips on Great Ovation at the national three-day event Championship at Deurne, Holland, in October 1970. This dressage performance earned them an interim 5th place, with 58.5 penalties; their final placing was 11th.

the Middlesex Hospital, a 54-year-old grandfather, a city insurance broker and a staff sergeant from the British army: 'It was a wonderful foursome.'

Curiously enough, the feeling of elation did not really return four years later at Munich, when Richard achieved his life's ambition and won the individual title together with his second team gold, on Derek Allhusen's brilliant gelding, Laurieston.

Everything was quite different. The weather was hot and dry, the going was firm and Britain had the hard task of defending the team gold medal. Richard was on a horse he had ridden for about nine months previously, Laurieston; and after they had finished 2nd at Badminton that year, Richard realized the horse had the ability to win, if only

Richard Meade and Barberry stood off for the Barrels at the Burghley three-day event World Championship in 1966 – and went on to take the individual silver medal.

inexperience did not lure him into doing something foolish. Richard says of him: 'Laurieston has a fascinating character; tough, intelligent, athletic, very able if he had a mind to be. He had been a stallion until he was five years old and the cussedness still showed sometimes – we enjoyed a sort of love-hate relationship.'

At Munich, Laurieston and Richard were chosen to go as number four for the team; a position of some heavy responsibility, as they might have to redress the balance of faults gained by an earlier team member. And as it turned out, that was what happened when Mark Phillips was unlucky enough to have two falls with Great Ovation on the cross-country course, so Laurieston had to go clear.

To witness Laurieston's dressage was quite an experience. As highly tuned as a violin for the exertions of the following day, he performed the movements of his dressage test like a volcano on the verge of eruption, and while some transitions were rather violent, the extensions were brilliantly and gracefully executed, displaying to the full the athleticism the horse was capable of. On the whole, the judges marked him somewhat leniently, giving him 50.67 penalties, a score that occasioned some harsh criticism from the Australian competitors. But, to their eternal credit, when Laurieston finally won the gold medal by a clear margin of 14 penalties, the Aussies were full of praise and said that he had won on merit, and by such a wide margin that it completely discounted the rather generous dressage score.

Richard's main worry on the cross-country course was a complex of fences starting at No. 21, and culminating in No. 23, a kind of Normandy Bank. 'Munich was a great challenge because there had been a lot of grief on the cross-country. The first three riders in the British team had all stopped at the 23rd fence in the third quarter of the course (which was by far the most difficult and contained all the problem fences; the last quarter was comparatively easy).

'There was a difficult take-off, which could be approached from either the left or the right side, preceded by a ditch into which horses could drop their legs. The top of the bank was 2 ft wider than the Normandy Bank at Badminton, and offered a choice of either one stride, for a horse with a great deal of scope, or, more probably, two strides, for a horse who lost impulsion or had less scope. Either way, it caused falls and refusals throughout the day.

'When I was about halfway round, I knew

I was fairly good for time, but I knew the next part would take some riding because Laurieston was not experienced. We were through the 23rd fence very quickly, however; he jumped it well – and we carried on as carefully as possible. The last $1^1/_4$ miles were a gallop for home: if the horse stayed on his feet, he could gallop on fast between the fences and steady up to jump them. Laurieston was a fast horse, but I had to steady up at fences because if I went fantastically fast, I could have had an upender, and thrown away the team chances. This is the difference between riding as an individual and being part of the team – you can't jeopardize the whole team effort. All the same, I went pretty fast and everything went absolutely fine until we came to three fences down the hill. There was a sort of escarpment with a fence at the top, another halfway down, then you went down to a green park bench at the bottom of the hill. If people were sitting on it, they would be facing away from you. The ground went down steeply, then levelled out.

'We were bowling on down the hill and I only just managed to get Laurieston back in time to steady up for the green bench. I thought for a nasty moment that I had lost control, but at the last second I managed it. After that, the final section of the course was a straightforward run for home – and a wonderful moment riding in at the end of the cross-country to find we had taken the lead for the team gold medal.' They had survived to gallop on to the finish in a fast time of $15^1/_2$ minutes, and take the individual lead with a 14-penalty advantage over the Italian, Alessandro Argentan and Woodland.

What mattered most was that the British team now took the lead over America, and this was, after all, what they had come to the

Always a force to be reckoned-with, attractive Mary Gordon-Watson here leaves the Badminton Lake in 1972 on Cornishman V.

Olympics for – to finish as a team. Bridget Parker and Cornish Gold were the only ones to collect 10 penalties in the final showjumping phase; and as both Mary Gordon-Watson on Cornishman, and Laurieston – who rattled the 2nd and 11th fences just to frighten everybody – went clear, they held on to take the gold medal.

'To win the individual gold medal should have been the high point of my life. And it sounds churlish to suggest that it somehow was not. But when I got home to England, it was Mexico I kept remembering, not Munich. The trouble was that for us, as the reigning Olympic team champions defending our title, Munich had not quite got the drama of Mexico. Or perhaps it was the team spirit, definitely with us in Germany, but not such a driving force as it had been in that unforgettable Mexican monsoon.

'But in retrospect, winning the team gold medal again and achieving my own goal with the individual title as well, meant an enormous amount. It took me rather a long time to realize that I had actually won the individual gold medal, and to feel the tremendous excitement of the whole thing.

'When we came back with nothing from Montreal, it made me value the ones I had much more! But I couldn't have possibly expected Jacob Jones to do any more than he did do at Bromont. In fact, after Badminton (1976), I thought that Jacob could finish in the top ten in Canada, but I was very thrilled when he was as close to the leaders as 4th – almost within reach of a medal. Being a big horse – he is over 17-hh – Jacob Jones has been very slow to mature, and also he lacks the natural attribute that so distinguished Laurieston: Jacob Jones is less quick away from his fences. Laurieston, who was under 16-hh, had tremendous acceleration; he would land after a fence and

you would be away so quickly that time could be saved that way, despite his comparative inexperience as an international horse.

'Pressure? Well, there is always pressure at the time of a major event, but possibly everyone reacts differently. I rather need a big competition to get the adrenalin flowing. In the time before the competition I try to lead as normal and relaxed a life as possible. I go for some training runs in the Park (Hyde Park, London) during the final fortnight – about a mile; I am more careful about what I eat, but I still do the usual things like having dinner with friends and going to the opera – music is a wonderful relaxation.'

Once upon a time Richard Meade was the youngster of the British three-day-event team, a youngster who had to prove himself worthy of a place beside elder, more accomplished horsemen. Now the pendulum has swung the opposite way – he is the veteran, well-experienced in international tactics, as secure as anybody ever is for a team place, and victor of some hard-fought battles. How do his team-mates rate him?

Jane Holderness-Roddam, who as Jane Bullen on Our Nobby rode with Richard in the gold-medal-winning team at Mexico, describes him as: 'undeniably one of the great eventers of all time. Experienced, he certainly is, after riding at his first event 18 years ago. But it is not just this, nor the hard work which he painstakingly puts into every horse he rides, but perhaps the total dedication to the sport and the perfection he has strived to achieve in every phase, which has produced his incredible record. Richard is always willing to learn from the experts and still seeks their help, concentrating most recently on the dressage, at present Britain's weakest phase. His

Wayfarer II was the mount of Richard Meade for the Dutch three-day event at Boekelo in October 1973.

showjumping, which cost him an individual gold medal back at the Tokyo Olympics in 1964, has now improved.

'Across country on the big day, Richard seldom makes a mistake, and has probably "recovered" from more "near misses" than any other rider. If he has yet to be really successful in bringing on a complete novice, his ability to bring on any horse from the halfway stage to a star at the top of the ladder is amazing.'

Jane's final tribute is perhaps the most significant: 'To me,' she says, 'Richard's greatest attribute is as a team member. His calmness during the event, his never-failing encouragement to his team-mates and his total dedication to the task ahead, are what have made him such a respected sportsman – not only among his fellow eventers but by all the equestrian world.'

Rodney Jenkins

Rodney Jenkins, born 3rd July 1944, in Orange, Virginia, is the leading professional rider in North America. His top horse, 14-year-old dark brown thoroughbred Idle Dice, has so far won more than $250,000 in prize money, a sum no European horse has even approached.

His father was a professional huntsman, so it is no surprise to learn that Jenkins spent a lot of his formative years in the hunting field, whipping-in to his father from the age of eleven. It was when he was 18 that he started competing in horse shows, and he was to turn professional shortly afterwards.

Since then he has slowly built up a stable of – including mares and foals – about 70 horses. It is not unusual to see him arrive at a show with more than a dozen horses, and during the course of it win with most of them. The US system of showing young horses in action over smallish fences makes it easy for a professional to have a number of rides in the same hunter class.

Red-haired Rodney was first asked to join USET in 1973, and in his first Nations Cup, at Washington, he had three clear rounds with Idle Dice to help the US team to victory. He has been in a further ten Nations Cups since then, and been on the winning side on seven occasions.

In 1974, he made his first competitive trip to Europe and finished 8th in the Men's World Championship at Hickstead with Idle Dice. In the Professional Championship at Cardiff that same year, he finished as runner-up to David Broome.

Even at a time when a new crop of talented young riders are winning regularly at the top American horse shows, the pair for whom the crowd reserve their most rapturous applause is the fiery red-headed Rodney Jenkins and his gallant partner, Idle Dice. The $250,000 in winnings this brilliant pair have amassed is even more staggering when one remembers that much of it was won in the early days of commercial interest in the sport in the United States, when the prize money on offer was far less than today.

In the United States, showjumping traditions die harder than in Europe and it was not until the North American Fall circuit of 1973, when Rodney was 29, that he was invited to jump as a member of the United States Equestrian Team. At the time, he said: 'I am a professional because the money I earn through horses provides my living, but I love a new challenge. For years in national classes I have wondered how I would fare internationally and the only way to meet the world's best is to be a USET member.' Riding Number One Spy at his first international representation at Washington, he was the only US rider to incur no penalties on the way to a home victory.

Ennis Jenkins, Rodney's father, has been his sole mentor. Ennis's devouring passion is hunting: he used to follow hounds as a boy, on a draught horse 'borrowed' from his father's farm. When Rodney was a child, Ennis had become huntsman for Manley Carter with the Rapidan Hounds at Orange, Virginia.

Rodney rode ponies from an early age, and experience in the hunting field helped to develop his great eye and taught him how to keep his weight back in the saddle. Today, when many of the leading showjumping riders employ extreme forward seats, Rodney's style is notable for his outstanding sense of balance and superb hands. Close scrutiny reveals that he holds his reins in a most unusual way, between his first and second fingers.

He did not really enjoy hunting, however, because for him it meant long days standing about in the icy winds of the severe Virginia winters, cleaning all the hunt horses when they returned home; and on school days, having to exercise at 6.00 am before setting off for the classroom.

Up till the time he was 18, Rodney rode in junior-division classes. He then had to decide whether to remain an amateur or become a professional show rider. But he says: 'There really was no decision to be made. I had to turn professional because I needed the money to help support my family. I now have professional status because my family were poor, so, in order to be able to jump, at least on the top national level, I had to be paid and provided with horses of the necessary scope and calibre for success. You have to have the motor in the right automobile in order to win. My biggest regret is that the Olympics are restricted to amateurs. It seems right out of touch with modern-style sport. Basically, one would like the best riders in the Games and it seems all wrong, for example, that David Broome could not take part in the Montreal Olympics, solely because he's professional. Shouldn't the Olympics – which are, if we are honest, the greatest prize of all – be contested by the ablest riders of the 20th century?'

The Jenkins family live, now as then, at Orange, Virginia – one of the few states where the horse is just as much a way of life as in the Heythrop or Beaufort Country in England. And the Orange County landscape, too, is reminiscent of Herefordshire: long, rolling hills and pastureland with woods of maple trees that turn to vivid orange, red and gold with the first sharp frost. The family own two farms, a total of approximately 200 acres, in a mixed farming area. Rodney makes no secret of the fact that he is happier at home than continually out on the national circuit.

He does not concentrate solely on top national or international jumpers. Indeed, few internationals have seen him in action in hunter classes, a field in which he excels, as his thirteen firsts in one day at Sedgefield, Carolina, in 1968 testify. If, in his opinion, a horse has jumping potential, Rodney seldom enters it in many hunter classes (a regular pattern in the States, where eight compulsory jumps are included in most classes) because, he considers, 'they take the cream off the hot chocolate'.

When Rodney was first invited to ride for USET he was completely thrilled. 'When the chance came,' he volunteers, 'I found it hard to believe.' Though he welcomed challenge, however, he found it particularly hard, after having so many chances in one class, to be confined to 'just one shot'.

It was the famed Idle Dice who provided Rodney with his passport to international competition. Rodney first saw Idle Dice on the Waterford racetrack, running with little enthusiasm. He had been bred in Kansas for racing on the flat and, on the day that Rodney first saw him, was a member of Irish trainer Dan Lannihan's Pennsylvania stables. 'I saw a big, dark brown gelding who was showing a total lack of interest in the job at hand, which was passing the winning post first. Instead, he was concentrating hard on watching the movements of the crowd.'

With the experience Rodney had now accumulated, he sensed that this was a horse of above average ability, the one he sought. His ideal is: 'a well-made, strong thoroughbred with big bones; powerful, short-backed and

Idle Dice and Rod Jenkins taking a spread in their stride during the summer visit to Britain in 1974.

naturally balanced.' Idle Dice stands 17-hh and fulfils all but one of Rodney's prerequisites: he is not short-backed.

Harry Gill, owner of a quarry business in Collegeville, Pennsylvania, and Rodney's biggest patron, bought Idle Dice; a move he has never regretted. 'Ike,' as the horse is known in the stable, was the first foal born to the stallion Haybrook, who is now also owned by Harry Gill. In 1968, when he was 5 years old, Idle Dice was shown in two Green Hunter classes and then directed immediately onto the indoor circuit, with instant success.

Since then, the partnership has become legendary, fulfilling Rodney's opinion, that 'great horses are good at everything – grand prix, speed and puissance,' by winning constantly in all three categories. Lesser horses – indeed, most horses – tend to specialize in one dimension.

'Idle Dice is very intelligent and wants to win just as much as I do, which is vital. Some horses may be just as good but not care as much. Equally, you could put wings on some horses and not get them over, they need to have heart.'

Rodney has experienced his greatest showjumping moments internationally, because 'there the challenge has been tougher and, to a degree, especially when in Europe, a journey into the unknown.'

'My first real thrill was winning the Washington Grand Prix for the President's Cup with "Ike" before I was first chosen for our team. National and international riders contest this grand prix, which on this occasion was held at the packed Armory Stadium in downtown Washington, and I had heard how great West German Hartwig Steenken and his mare Simona were – although this was before they won the World Championship in 1974. I had closely watched Hartwig schooling Simona

and quickly realized what a superb workman he was. When we both reached the jump-off, I didn't rate my chance at all well although I had decided to have a go. Hartwig and Simona went first and jumped a fantastic clear, which to me seemed unbeatable. I could not believe my ears as I crossed the finishing line and heard the announcer saying that I had beaten Simona by five seconds; it just seemed impossible. I was just trying to break into the international scene – and you remember your first good international win better than any other.'

Rodney went on to prove that this was no fluke victory by beating Simona on a further four occasions on the North American circuit.

'Being part of a team is an experience I love, partly because I had to wait so long for it. When I come into the ring, I feel as though I'm battling for civil rights. That first year I rode, in 1973, we had a good Fall circuit – USET won at Washington, New York and Toronto. The team coach, Bert de Nemethy, is always very keen that we should do well at these North American shows and there is a great team spirit.'

When Rodney was chosen as a USET member in 1974, for the team to compete against Europe which would include the World Championship, it meant that the ambition of a lifetime was fulfilled. 'One crucial error which cost me a genuine World Championship shot was made before I even left the States.' Advice was offered to him from many sources, but, with a busy stable and owners anxious about their hunters if he was to be away in Europe three months, he finally chose to go only to Great Britain, with a warm-up show at Kent County before the opening day of the July Hickstead meeting where the World Championship was being staged. The rest of USET – Frank Chapot, Robert Ridland, Kathy Kusner, Mike Matz together with Dennis

Ex-US team captain Bill Steinkraus on Main Spring shows the Lucerne spectators how to clear the water with ease; they won the Preis Gübelin.

Murphy and Buddy Brown who were having their first experience of the European circuit — made an extended Continental tour, being based in Germany and competing at such shows as Aachen and La Baule to get fully acclimatized and settled by Hickstead.

Rodney's European début was not his most memorable experience. Fighting jet-lag, he also had to endure a real torrential downpour throughout the two-day Kent County Show, which proved a worthless and depressing initiation. At Hickstead, all the top riders, Harvey Smith, Alwin Schockemöhle, Eddie Macken, Hartwig Steenken, Nelson

Pessoa, Hugo Arrambide, Captain Raimondo d'Inzeo and the reigning champion, David Broome, had gathered to fight for the title. With many European riders now declared professional, the title was even more closely contended than usual as it would clearly be more beneficial in terms of advertising revenue.

As Rodney describes it: 'The rules were so different from any showing I had done previously. Having to prepare only one horse rather than two proved part of my undoing, and then, when it was too late, I realized exactly what each article meant.'

'In the first speed class, I blew the whole thing when I finished well down the line. If I had been 9th or even 10th I would still have had some chance of making the final four-horse ride-off. I had not realized the importance of placing well in every competition for the all-over points system. The crowd always upsets Idle Dice, who is very highly strung and emotional. It's a vicious circle; he's so popular that they clap and call as soon as they see him come into the ring, and during the round, and it often diverts his attention from the jumps. It was just as it had been on that day when I first saw him at the racecourse, when he had seemed to be paying little attention to the job on hand: again, he was apprehensive, sensing a big occasion and uneasy on a strange showground. With the towering Derby Bank and permanent jumps, it was quite different from anything in the US at the time; although we now have almost a replica, with Mason Phelps' permanent American Jumping Derby Course on Rhode Island.

'The jumps were not comparable to anything I'd ever tackled before. You need a very brave horse to win at Hickstead and I realized too late that it would have been a real help to have been used to them before the championship itself.'

Rodney, who had always thought that if he could possibly reach the jump-off (in which the four remaining riders ride first their own and then each other's horses) 'it would be real fun', missed the chance; most unfortunately, from the spectators' point of view, since a considerable part of Rodney's success owes to his ability to understand and quickly adapt to different horses.

'When you feel as down as I did after the World Championship – and Idle Dice, who was unquestionably my best horse at the time, just wasn't showing his best form – the going becomes really tough. I welcomed a change of scene and the journey up to the Empire Pool at Wembley, in London, for the Royal International Horse Show; although many other competitors grumbled about going indoors mid-season.

'Towards the end of the week, Number One Spy, my second horse, a chestnut thoroughbred whom I can rely on never to stop, and know that if he hits a fence, more often than not, it will be only one, was running into form.

'The John Player Grand Prix of Great Britain was on the Friday night, but as I walked the track I wasn't too optimistic. It wasn't because the jumps were too big but because the course didn't really seem to flow. Fifteen of us got through to the second round, and seven remained for the final barrage against the clock: two for West Germany, three for Great Britain and Buddy (Brown) and myself for the US.' The course was now enormous for an indoor arena, ending in vertical poles at 5 ft 6 in.

'Buddy opened on Sandsablaze and finished in 40.5 seconds. Hartwig Steenken, on Simona, caught a pole coming out of the treble,

United States representatives Idle Dice and Rodney Jenkins are shown in the third qualifying competition of the 1974 Men's World Championship at Hickstead, Sussex.

then Number One Spy took me into the lead with a sharp clear which no one bettered. David Broome finished runner-up on another American-bred former racehorse, the grey Philco.

'David, who was on the British team that competed in the States in 1973, has become a real friend of mine. As we rode into the ring that day to collect our awards, he said: "There you are – now you are a hero for 24 hours." That's a pretty good saying and so true. I was on top of the world because I'd scored my first major victory in Great Britain and it is a night I will never forget.

'The international riders are pretty nice people. On a given day they can whip you and they all try to win all the time. Harvey Smith, who had failed to win his seventh British grand prix the previous night but was presented with a special trophy to commemorate his six previous victories (the first at the White City in 1965 with Harvester), showed us all the way home in the final big class, the Victor Ludorum, with the German horse Salvador. David Broome was runner-up for the second consecutive night and I was out of the money. David's words had come true all too soon.'

Like most showjumping riders, Rodney has experienced the good as well as the bad days. Because he is one of the world's best, he returned to the top despite a somewhat daunting 1976 season, about which he says: 'I know some time you have to have bad news, but I never fell off so many times in my whole life as I did that year! I seemed to be struggling all the time.'

In September, he separated his shoulder from his collar-bone in a fall at an indoor show at Providence, Rhode Island. Nevertheless, he ended the week-long Washington CSIO by sharing the grand prix for the President's Cup (on Number One Spy) with Terry Rudd, a girl

he regularly helped on Mr. Demeanour, whom he often rode himself. Tragically, Mr. Demeanour had to be put down after fracturing knee joint bones when warming up in the collecting ring at Cleveland, Ohio, in September, 1977, before the puissance.

The week after Washington, at the opening of the New York CSIO at Madison Square Garden, Rodney took a horrid fall from the French thoroughbred Viscount, who had been ridden by Frank Chapot in the Montreal Olympics. This time, Rodney fractured bones in the same collar-bone/upper-arm area and so ended his chances of further competition in 1976.

It takes a champion to come back after a nasty fall and 1977 did not begin on an auspicious note, when, in the spring, Number One Spy damaged a hind leg jumping off a sandy surface on the Florida circuit, and so put himself out of action for the entire season. This meant that Rodney had to rely on Idle Dice for all the top 1977 competitions. Among the other horses he was riding, Prime Time is a fantastic speed specialist, while Mrs. Theodore Gaston's powerful big Icy Paws, who finished 3rd in the Philadelphia Gold Cup, needed experience.

Although this put too much pressure on Idle Dice, it was also to give Rodney one of his most rewarding moments in showjumping. His main 1977 target was to win the Grand Prix Championship. This is awarded to the leading rider on one horse on a points system, covering most of the major US grand prix and ending with the President's Cup at Washington. By the time the final grand prix came up, Idle Dice headed the list, marginally ahead of another professional pair, Bernie Traurig and The Cardinal, whose uncomfortably close

Crowd-puller Rod Jenkins, watched by an intent press corps, competing on Idle Dice in the 1974 Men's World Championship at Hickstead, Sussex.

attendance meant the issue was by no means settled. If Idle Dice were unplaced and Bernie Traurig won, The Cardinal would be the 1977 Grand Prix Champion of the United States.

Course-builder Pamela Carruthers had left before the final class for Teheran, leaving behind the exact specifications for the grand prix course. It seemed likely that one or two minor alterations had been made because the odd jump did not quite ride as freely as Pamela's jumps usually ride. As it turned out, however, the course had no bearing on the result of the Grand Prix Championship. Neither The Cardinal nor Idle Dice was involved in the final barrage, which was won by Buddy Brown and Sandsablaze; and this meant that Idle Dice was the 1977 Grand Prix Champion.

'I was so very proud when I led Idle Dice in to receive that award. During the season, people had been saying he was finished and was done with, but they forget he's not been played with, he's been jumped, really jumped, for nine years running. Then, in his 14th summer, he had this real tough season because Spy was side-lined. Idle Dice was very consistent in the grand prix series; he was in the ribbons at all but two, and in one of these, he slipped and fell when clean two fences from home.

'Idle Dice is a proud horse, too, and wants to go clear. It's always easy to know when he's tired because he gets grumpy in his box but he still gives his very best in the ring.

'The worst thing for the future is that I judge others I buy by Ike – and that way, it's all too easy to miss a real nice horse.'

Eddie Macken

Born on October 20th 1949, in Granard, County Longford, Eddie Macken is the youngest of five children, four boys and a girl. His father, who runs a butcher's shop in Granard, is also a farmer with an interest in horses. Eddie's education began at a school run by nuns; but his parents decided that he was being treated too mercifully and dispatched him to a Catholic boarding school in the capital town of Longford. He recalls: 'My parents thought it would be good for my training if they sent me to boarding school, to harden me up and make a man out of me. I don't think they succeeded. I hated school and, against everybody's wishes, I pulled out before the end of my time there, without taking the leaving certificate.'

Eddie's riding education, in happy contrast, was to be marked by conspicuous success. Taught by his father, Jimmy Macken, to ride, Eddie started hunting – on a small black-and-white pony that cost his father £47.10s – with the Longford Harriers when he was five years old. He began competing in junior jumping classes around 1960, on a 13.2-hh pony, Granard Boy, and progressed to the 14.2-hh classes with Granard Lad.

After his premature departure from boarding school, he spent two years helping his father in the family business; and in return, his father helped with the breaking-in of the ponies and young horses Eddie took to local jumping competitions or the hunting field. He never tried to emulate his oldest brother, a soldier in Dublin, who used to try his skill riding at flapper meetings and point-to-points: 'I'm too cowardly for that,' says Eddie, 'and anyway, I'm too heavy.' (He is six feet tall and weighs 13 stone.) But Eddie found he had a natural instinct for riding: a gift that attracted the notice of Iris Kellett, the international showjumper who was to win the 1969 Ladies' European Championship in Dublin and retire immediately afterwards.

Eddie went to Iris Kellett's Dublin establishment early in 1969. After her retirement, later in the year, she handed on to him her international partner, Morning Light, and it was on this horse that Eddie made his début with the Irish team in the next season. Other horses also aided Eddie's rapid ascent of the international ladder: Maxwell, Oatfield Hills, Easter Parade and, most notably, Pele, who proved his own class as well as that of his rider by taking the World Championship silver medal at Hickstead in 1974.

Early in 1975, Eddie was given a professional licence by the Irish Federation – and made headlines by opting to leave the Kellett stables and ride in Germany for oil-magnate Dr. Herbert Schnapka. The Irish connection (Schnapka, who owns horses ridden by leading Germans such as Hartwig Steenken and Paul Schockemöhle, also owns the Ferrans Stud, outside Kilcock, Co. Kildare) ensures that Eddie can comply with the Irish rule that states that he must ride an Irish-bred and Irish-owned horse at a CSIO (official international) horse show.

Eddie's partnership with Pele was resumed early in 1977, when the Irish Dairy Board leased him from Miss Kellett – and renamed him, Kerrygold. But Eddie's real money-spinner has been the Irish-bred Boomerang.

The year of 1976 was a record one for a particular globe-trotting Irishman, Eddie Macken. From the time the curtain went up at Hickstead, before Easter, until his final bow at Olympia prior to Christmas, Eddie, in a virtually unbroken run of success that left his rivals breathless and the sports journalists bereft of superlatives, scored nearly 30 major international victories in Europe and America to become the world's leading rider. He won in Rome, Wiesbaden, Cardiff, Hamburg, Hickstead, Wembley, Dublin, Rotterdam, Donaueschingen, Hickstead, Aachen, Wembley, Washington, New York, Toronto and Olympia. Most of his successes were with the Irish gelding Boomerang, who claimed over three-quarters of the overall prize money of around £35,000.

Within two short years of winning his World Championship silver medal, which virtually coincided with his emergence as a fully-fledged international competitor, Eddie had ridden to a commanding position in Europe that was equalled only by the Olympic triumph of his present nextdoor neighbour in Germany, Alwin Schockemöhle.

How, one marvels, could it all have happened so quickly? A clue may lie in the spectacle of this well-built, 26-year-old Irishman at work with a horse: Eddie Macken is moulded into the saddle in classic style, the sympathetic movement of his hands barely perceptible even from a short distance. 'A born horseman,' Hans Günther Winkler once said of him; but the very first to recognize this gift was an Irish lady rider, Iris Kellett. She was in her last season as an international competitor when she discovered Eddie – and to her must go the credit for the shaping of a star.

'I went to Iris in January 1969, when she was in her last year as a rider with Morning Light, and it was very lucky for me that I did,

because I got the breaks – I took over the good horses from her when she retired. I got Morning Light the next season, 1970; he was the first horse I rode in the international arena at Dublin. But for about a year, Iris was a very hard teacher. She would hardly let me ride across the school without coming to see that I was doing it properly.'

Iris Kellett's wonderful flair for teaching, knowing when to watch, when to counsel and when to instruct, developed Eddie's natural feel and balance into a skill that has since taken him into the select ranks of horsemen who were once his heroes: 'Like Billy Steinkraus and Peter Robeson: lovely horsemen for me to watch, so fluent, so smooth, so brilliant. Or Raimondo (d'Inzeo): so effective, really the tops.' She taught him to be patient: 'Like everybody else, I love to get up and jump and jump and jump. But you have to do a certain amount of groundwork. Easter Parade had to have a lot of that. His problem was always temperament; he stopped and napped and was a little bit tricky, but he could do gymnastics: shoulder in, extended and collected movements, turns on the forehand, half passes; he was a very athletic horse, very supple naturally and this helped enormously for indoor jumping. He tended to be over-collected, so I had to get him to extend, lengthen his neck and stride.'

After a season with Morning Light (during which Eddie made his Nations Cup début in the Aga Khan Trophy at Dublin), the horse was sold to France for a reputed £30,000, and eventually replaced by Oatfield Hills. Together with Easter Parade, the stable newcomer from Galway began to build up quite a reputation in Ireland for Eddie; and by 1972, the major home championships were all coming his way: Galway, Westport, Cork – and Strokestown, which stuck in Eddie's memory somewhat dramatically.

'This was the car that I won and lost. I had four horses qualified for the championship at Strokestown, but I could only jump three. They put up a car for the winner of the competition at first, and then our showjumping federation kicked up a fuss and said: "You can't do this – the 2nd prize has to be in such a relation to the 1st." They were determined to give the car, so they said: "Right, we'll give it to the rider." And then the federation said: "If the rider accepts the car, he'll be turned professional"; but nothing more came of this. I won the car in the end – on a mare called Brown Admiral, a half-sister of Oatfield Hills

(out of the same dam) – but I hadn't much luck with it. It was a good car, but I had this slight mishap, when a wall jumped out in front of us one night; and that was that!'

The following year came the Men's European Championship at Hickstead. Eddie Macken's name was not high on the list of favourites, with such stars as Alwin Schockemöhle and Paddy McMahon taking part, but it was reckoned that he stood a good outsider's chance with his promising record behind him. But Easter Parade, one of his two rides at Hickstead, had other ideas, as Eddie recalls gloomily: 'Occasionally, I had problems with Easter Parade, who was a horse that didn't trust anybody at first, and I had to win his

Eddie Macken, here on Spring Time, jumping at Lucerne in May 1976.

confidence back. On that first day at Hickstead, he let me down at the first fence. He stopped at the first fence, and that did me for the whole Championship, because Oatfield Hills wasn't that type of horse; he was not a speed horse as such. He couldn't have a really good fast go at that type of Table C track; whereas Easter Parade was very athletic, very sharp, very quick and I was banking on him to have a good time that day. In fact, after the first fence I lost a lot of time, although he had a very good round.

'It was a very bad start – first horse, first fence, first day, and I lost a lot of confidence

The efforts of Hugo Simon and Flipper earned a win for Austria in the Hickstead, Sussex, Grand Prix in April 1976.

Pele and Eddie Macken at the Men's World Championship at Hickstead, Sussex, in July 1974, during the final.

after that. It had been hard enough when Iris and I arrived at Hickstead; I felt a bit down as there were a lot of very experienced people there, the opposition was so great. But, looking back on it, I think we should have tried to arrange a big show in England before going to Hickstead, because we jumped at home on the Sunday before, over a course Iris and I thought for a national course was quite big.

'But when we came to Hickstead, there was no comparison. The fences there were much bigger, much more difficult, with the result that, as the week went on, the horses improved and I improved, but it was just too

46

late. It took us the first two days to get going, and the first day spoiled it, because though Oatfield Hills finished equal 2nd or 3rd on the second day, and he jumped quite well on the last day which would have put us well in with a chance, I had been left behind too far at the start to ever catch up. We finished 9th eventually, a bit of a let-down.

'You see, in Ireland, the courses are so small, and the opposition was not on the same scale as it is in England and on the Continent. That year Easter Parade had won something like £1,300 before he came over to Hickstead for the Championship, and in Ireland that takes a lot of winning. In Britain, for example, Pennwood Forge Mill could have been winning £8,000–£10,000 in the same year that Oatfield Hills would have won £2,000 if he was lucky.'

Hickstead had been a crushing disappointment; but Eddie hit the headlines immediately afterwards at the Royal International Horse Show at Wembley by winning the Moss Bros. Puissance on Oatfield Hills. He vividly describes his feelings of the moment: 'The first time I ever really got keyed up over a competition was that night at Wembley. It was the first time I had ever ridden down to a fence of 7 ft 1 in – and the first time I had ever been in the final of a big competition at a big show. I'd say, I was a bit keyed up over it, and certainly so scared, it was hard to realize it was all happening.'

It was at Dublin that August that Eddie mentioned a very promising horse in Iris Kellett's stable that he was riding: 'There is a very good young horse at home, Pele. Now *he* is really something. But I expect someone will pick him up during Dublin – a rich Italian? Fiona Kinnair is the owner, and she'll have to sell him if she gets an offer of £40,000. Ireland is a dealing nation, and if we sell nothing but

the bad ones, we'll have nobody coming to us to buy horses. But I'm all for keeping the horses, and we could if only we had proper sponsorship. If anyone was to buy Pele to stay in Ireland, the Army should; they need a good horse.'

As it turned out, happily for Eddie's future, Iris Kellett had no intention of letting Pele go, even as far as out of her own gate. She bought him, so that Eddie could continue a most promising partnership; one to which the rest of the world payed homage a year later, when the Men's World Championship was staged at Hickstead. Looking back on that momentous occasion, Eddie remembers: 'My first victory at Wembley was the Moss Bros. Puissance with Oatfield Hills. Wembley's such a place to win at. It was the first really big international class I had ever won – I had been to Wembley before, but this was all much bigger, bigger fences and everything. It meant something to me, to win then.

'But the World Championship was fantastic. To win the class on the first day: I was as much surprised as anyone else. The second qualifier, the puissance; that was something. Pele had never jumped puissance before. It was all a fantastic build-up. I had to be happy with the result, but I had to kick myself afterwards; I didn't think I was going to win in the final. The third qualifier was the Nations Cup class: I had a clear round and 4 faults at the last part of the combination – this was on the third day – and it was the only fence Pele had down in the three qualifiers.

'Pele came to Hickstead at the spring meeting of that year (1974), and went very well. The problem in Ireland is that if you go winning national classes there, that is not the same thing as jumping at Hickstead; as I had already found out the year before, when I came for the European Championship. I had jumped

Boy (Eddie Macken) at the beginning of the course for the Dick Turpin Stakes, part of the October 1976 Horse of the Year Show, Wembley, London.

Pele at national shows in Ireland, but they are not big fences at home. And schooling with Iris, I didn't jump over big fences either, usually, unless there was some special problem. But after seeing Hickstead that spring, I put up one or two big combinations in training. That was Pele's weakness, if anything.

'I walked the course on the first day of the Championships, and I liked the way it was built. Everything flowed on. The puissance, the second day, was enormous and I was first to jump. In the second round, I never thought that four inches could make such a difference to a fence in my life. The first round had been like this:

No. 1 a wall $\left(5 \text{ ft } 0^{1}/_{4} \text{ in x } 5 \text{ ft } 3 \text{ in}\right)$

No. 2 vertical rails on very big pillars $\left(5 \text{ ft } 5^{1}/_{2} \text{ in}\right)$

No. 3 parallel oxer, planks in front and rails at the back $\left(4 \text{ ft } 9 \text{ in}/5 \text{ ft } 1^{1}/_{2} \text{ in x } 6 \text{ ft } 6^{3}/_{4} \text{ in}\right)$

No. 4 triple bar $\left(3 \text{ ft } 8^{1}/_{2} \text{ in}/4 \text{ ft } 8 \text{ in}/ 5 \text{ ft } 9 \text{ in x } 6 \text{ ft } 7^{1}/_{2} \text{ in}\right)$

No. 5 another vertical $\left(5 \text{ ft } 7 \text{ in}\right)$

No. 6 a big oxer, planks and rails $\left(5 \text{ ft } 1^{1}/_{2} \text{ in}/ 5 \text{ ft } 7 \text{ in x } 6 \text{ ft } 1 \text{ in}\right)$

No. 7 another parallel-type oxer $\left(5 \text{ ft } 1^{3}/_{4} \text{ in}/ 5 \text{ ft } 9 \text{ in x } 6 \text{ ft } 6^{3}/_{4} \text{ in}\right)$

No. 8 a straight wall $\left(5 \text{ ft } 7 \text{ in}\right)$.

'When it came to the second round, the jump-off, No. 5 and No. 6 fences were taken out and the rest were all put up four inches, so the course went like this:

Little wall

Vertical rails

Parallel oxer – Pele was afraid over that, and got his hind legs into the middle, then whipped them up again.

Triple bar – I was lucky there. I let Pele run on to get him going forward again.

Another parallel-type oxer – the biggest on the course. Pele jumped it very well.

Last fence, the straight wall – high, but we had the right-handed turn from the big oxer before it, to steady us up. Pele cleared it without any problem, and we were home.

'At that stage, it looked pretty sure I was going to qualify unless something terrible happened. Then came the last qualifier, Nations Cup day, over a very big course.

The combination had related distances in the last line of fences, starting with

No. 12 Parallel oxer $\left(4 \text{ ft } 10^{1}/_{4} \text{ in}/5 \text{ ft } 1^{1}/_{2} \text{ in x } 6 \text{ ft } 6^{3}/_{4} \text{ in}\right)$

then five or six strides to the combination:

No. 13a Brush and rail – 4 ft $10^{1}/_{2}$ in with a distance of 25 ft $2^{1}/_{2}$ in to the next element:

No. 13b Oxer $\left(4 \text{ ft } 9 \text{ in}/5 \text{ ft } 0^{1}/_{4} \text{ in x } 6 \text{ ft } 2^{3}/_{4} \text{ in}\right)$ with a distance of 24 ft 9 in to the last element:

No. 13c Brush oxer $\left(4 \text{ ft } 11^{1}/_{2} \text{ in}/5 \text{ ft } 1^{3}/_{4} \text{ in x } 6 \text{ ft } 6^{3}/_{4} \text{ in}\right)$

and that's when everyone got into trouble.

'Five strides from the parallels to the first part of the combination could mean you did not jump in far enough, with enough impulsion to get out safely over the big spreads of the second and third part. Six strides from the parallels to the start of the combination could be right, but could put you too far in, and you would be under the first spread and in trouble. A lot of people, I think, under-estimated it when they walked it; but I had known Pele had problems and had worked on them. We got through the combination with 4 faults at the last part, and we were easily through to the final. Those 4 faults meant that Hartwig Steenken (and Simona) took over from me the place of leading qualifier, but it didn't matter as we all started even on the last day.'

The first round of the final left all four protagonists level-pegging with clear rounds on their own horses. In the second round, Frank Chapot had No. 6 down with Hugo Simon's Lavendel, and Eddie faulted at the same fence, an oxer, on Chapot's Main Spring. 'I shouldn't have had that one down,' Eddie remembers now. 'I could have kicked myself. I didn't react quick enough. I had watched Frank riding him, but when you get on a strange horse you have to feel; you can't imitate. But I felt the most at home with Main Spring.'

To finish the second round, Steeken was clear with Pele, and Simon hit No. 6 for 4 faults with Simona. Steenken thus went ahead, but in the third round, Eddie and Chapot caught up. The Irishman was clear on Lavendel, a masterly display of control; Steenken hit No. 6 on Main Spring, for 4 faults; Simon dropped back with a mistake on Pele at the water; but Chapot level-pegged with a breathtakingly fast clear on Simona. The fourth round saw Steenken maintaining his place with a slightly edgy round on Lavendel, Simon faultless on Main Spring, but Chapot falling back to join Hugo Simon when Pele landed right in the water. Then Eddie had to equal Hartwig Steenken on the headstrong Simona, who seemed determined to go at full speed throughout, having clearly had enough of strange jockeys; but the pair came home faultless, with Eddie hanging on for dear life, to force a jump-off.

Eddie takes up the story: 'We changed back to our own horses, and I was first to go again. I think I would have been better off if I hadn't been first, as I would have known what to beat, but with Simona to follow me, I had to

An intent Eddie Macken (Pele) is on his way to finishing runner-up in the 1974 Men's World Championship at Hickstead, Sussex.

go as fast as I could. Pele had the No. 6 down, and then the water. Until that day, Pele had never been in the water in his life but after two mistakes at it with two strange riders in the space of minutes, he had discovered he need not bust himself to clear it, and that was that. If we hadn't had 4 faults there, I could have beaten Hartwig (4 faults also in the water with Simona), who had a slower time. I think we all

expected the fences to be big in that jump-off, after the enormous ones in the qualifiers, but it was not so. One thing about the changing-of-horses pattern – I think it would be a better test if everybody rode four strange horses that nobody had seen or known before. But altogether, it was a fantastic end to the thing;

The European Amateur Championship in 1975 was held at Munich, where Hartwig Steenken on Erle came second in the Individual placings.

I had to pinch myself to realise I was really runner-up for the World Championship.'

At La Baule, four years earlier, there had been two rest days before the final; at Hickstead, there was only one. But in either case, here was definitely an opportunity for a rider to become heavily pressurized by the waiting. Eddie comments: 'Tommy Brennan and I were discussing this at a party one night.

If you live showjumping, never take a drink, go to bed early every night, and have it for breakfast, dinner and tea, you are under pressure all the time. But if you have a drink, go to a party, you forget about the whole thing and there is not half the pressure on you.'

Opinions on taking a drink before a

A boyhood hero: Seamus Hayes, here on Doneraile, at the 1966 Royal International Horse Show.

competition are sharply divided: Alison Dawes used to claim she always rode better on a brandy and a late night, and Olympic eventing champion Richard Meade likes to take a glass of wine before a big day. But some maintain it puts the 'eye' out and impairs reflexes. Eddie himself says: 'You may wake up next morning with a sore head; but it stops you worrying about something else. I'm all for enjoying myself – I like heated swimming pools, and a party with a good sing-song.'

Nevertheless, Eddie keeps himself fit: he used to play Gaelic football, before he put out his knee, and likes to play with the hurley stick, or badminton when he can. 'But I ride so much that I keep fairly fit that way,' he says. 'In Ireland, if you went away to a weekend show you had a good time, a party, you enjoyed yourself. But now in England and in Germany it has become big business, so you have to keep on the ball. It's all professional.'

Eddie gave up the Olympic dream when the Irish Federation turned him professional. He took advantage of this by accepting an offer to ride in Germany, where he is based with the Schockemöhle brothers; though he still rides under the Irish flag. He has joined the world that seemed so inaccessible when he was a small boy building castles in the air.

'I can remember – it's funny. When I was a kid on ponies, I used to watch Seamus (Hayes) on Goodbye and Tommy (Wade) on Dundrum, sitting in my chair in front of the television. I used to go to bed at night and I'd be jumping big walls, I'd be jumping fences all night in my sleep, dreaming about it. I never came over to England then, but it's funny looking back on it. It's something you'd never dream about, never dream that one day I'd be in that company.'

HRH The Princess Anne

HRH Princess Anne, born 15th August 1950, second child of HM Queen Elizabeth II, might well have been expected to confine her equestrian activities to those least likely to occasion the risk of personal injury. Instead she took up the sport of eventing and, with the help of top-class trainer Alison Oliver, won the European championship with Doublet barely four years after starting in her first official event.

There had been outings at Pony Club level prior to that; but her almost meteoric rise to top-level competition owes much to encouragement from her parents, both of whom are first-class riders. Indeed, had Doublet, who was bred as a polo pony for Prince Philip, not grown to 16.2 hh and thus been given to her to event, there might have been a different tale to tell.

The princess's first three-day event was at Tidworth, where she finished well down the field with Purple Star. Doublet carried her to 5th place in her first Badminton outing, in 1971 – the winner being her future husband on Great Ovation. As a result of her placing, Princess Anne was invited to ride as an individual in the 1971 European Horse Trials at Burghley.

She finished that event as Champion of Europe – and many of those who had scoffed at her riding ability were converted. At the Trout Hatchery, the princess could so easily have landed in the rather pungent water; but she slipped the reins, let him get his head – and the situation was saved.

Doublet did not appear the following year, owing to tendon trouble; and three refusals in the final 1973 trial at Osberton denied him Kiev. So ex-showjumper Goodwill carried her in defence of the title at Kiev, only to fall at the treacherous No. 2 fence.

Goodwill finished 5th at Badminton in 1974, but Doublet had performed a top-rate dressage test, only to fall on the steeplechase course. A few weeks later, while being schooled in Windsor Great Park, Doublet fractured a hind hock and had to be put down.

This left the princess with Goodwill to ride in the individual World Championship at Burghley, where she finished 12th.

For the 1975 European Championship, the princess had the satisfaction of being in an all-women British team. With Goodwill, she gained the individual silver medal, in addition to a team silver that might have been a gold had Harley and Sue Hatherly not fallen in the showjumping phase.

Goodwill proved himself fit enough to go to Bromont, where the three-day event of the Montreal Olympics was held. There, his rider finished in 24th place, having shown the customary female 'guts' by continuing after a bad fall at the 19th cross-country fence.

At the beginning of the 1977 season it was announced that the princess was expecting a child and would not compete. She and Captain Phillips now live in Gloucestershire where they have set up their own training establishment.

Although Princess Anne tries hard to group her official duties away from the main spring and autumn horse trials, she seldom manages more than four consecutive days training. Accordingly, her breakthrough onto the international scene came as a surprise to all; and to no-one more than herself.

Princess Anne was not an experienced event rider and still learning when she first rode Doublet, himself a green horse who had been ridden in his first trial by trainer Alison Oliver. His owner found him hard to get to know: he was tremendously aloof and in the stable just stood and gazed out of the door. For a long time she felt she was making no progress; and certainly had not expected to win the first time she rode him in competition, at Osberton in Nottinghamshire. In 1971, she rode at Badminton for the first time, finishing 5th. This performance earned her and Doublet a place on the short-list to compete as individuals in the European Championship at Burghley the following September.

After an unexpected operation and spell in hospital in July 1971, Princess Anne convalesced in Scotland, walking up and down the hills round Balmoral, then exercising as much as possible on the Royal Yacht. She was utterly determined to ride at Burghley, if it were humanly possible: 'All along, I felt I'd get fit in time. I had already decided that if anything hurt, it would be wise to call it a day and in that respect, I was lucky.

'Beforehand, I considered my chances fair, in terms of finishing the competition; and had no real ambition beyond that. When I got there, needless to say, I thought it was the biggest course I had ever seen. I was worried about the spreads because I didn't feel they were Doublet's strong point.'

At the conclusion of the dressage phase, the combination held the lead. Princess Anne recalls: 'On cross-country day, after he'd jumped the first fence, it was patently obvious he was out to enjoy himself. I'd had a very good steeplechase round on time, which I'd managed without causing myself too much strain or fear. Doublet was obviously really fit and recovered quickly afterwards, which was encouraging. It was a very remarkable ride. I'd never had such a trouble-free round, apart from the hiccup coming out of the Trout Hatchery. I don't think I've ever had such a good ride since, other than at Luhmühlen with Goodwill. Although I wasn't going very fast, it was an extraordinarily smooth trip.'

It was an extremely economical performance; although the Princess says, effacingly: 'It was more my good luck than good judgement, because I hadn't the experience to know how fast I was going; but I knew that every time I reached a fence and said, "Now, Doublet, pay attention," he did. One of his great strengths was his accuracy, jumping corners and at angles.'

Princess Anne had a substantial lead prior to the final showjumping but was not convinced that this would help her at all. 'The previous twenty-four hours were horrible. When I actually realized I was in the lead, I was in a state of suspension, knowing that I should be able to go clear perfectly easily – but could I? Showjumping makes me feel ill; I find it very trying. It's immediately obvious to people what is going on. Having done a lot of hard work, a tiny little mistake can be magnified and make you look a complete idiot and that is rather depressing, especially if you went well across country. Doublet was not the world's greatest showjumper, but he always managed to rise to the occasion.' At Burghley, a faultless round secured her the European gold medal.

Although the record books confirm this victory as the Princess's greatest achievement

to date, she does not concur: 'Because other people had done so much towards it, especially Alison Oliver, who was my trainer at the time, I didn't realize quite what an achievement it was.'

To Princess Anne, Goodwill's silver medal in the 1975 European Championship at Luhmühlen, near Lüneburg, in Germany, gave her the greatest sense of achievement and satisfaction to date. 'It may seem rather curious, because I was second to Lucinda Prior-Palmer and Be Fair, but it was because by then I knew what I was doing and that Goodwill had become a completely different horse.'

Initially, he had been very uptight: 'There were occasions we despaired that he'd ever do anything much in the dressage arena; his showjumping was erratic and sketchy and he got very carried away; but his cross-country was never any trouble. My only problem there was that his weight was very much on his forehand and I got very tired, trying to get his head off the ground so as to approach the fences with a certain amount of control and balance.'

This difficulty was partially solved with the use of a gag, which moved his centre of gravity sufficiently to eradicate the problem and the Princess now rarely uses the gag. It took time, however, and has altered his whole way of crossing country. He now moves and gallops far better than before.

'One of the hazards with his dressage was the experimental test we had one year, which included a flying change that came far too soon for him. He thought it meant showjumping and one lost him completely and hardly dared to do it. Without doubt, arenas and large collections of people definitely worried him; but it's hard to know, with a horse, whether it's excitement or fear. Now he's less affected

Goodwill, with HRH The Princess Anne, enjoying fine weather for the dressage test at Luhmühlen early in September 1975.

in that he will listen to you, but you can still feel him change visibly underneath you. In the Olympics at Bromont, he did it as he entered the arena, which had been hidden by a surrounding bank, and was presented with a sudden mass of people and noise. They took him completely by surprise and he completely froze and said, "I want to go home".'

At Badminton in 1973, Goodwill finished 8th and earned himself a place on the short-list for the European Championship at Kiev, which enabled the Princess to defend her title. The size of the fences at Kiev seemed unlikely to trouble Goodwill. The only doubt was his lack of experience: he had contested only one three-day event. He began by going brilliantly round the steeplechase course, well within the time.

'At the start of the cross-country, I'm usually a bit jazzed up; it's a mistake if you aren't. But on this occasion, I didn't feel anything, which is a bad sign and usually means something may go wrong.' The Princess arrived in a swirling cloud of dust at the notorious fence No. 2, a spread of solid poles over a deep, wide ditch after the descent of a steep hill with little approach room. Here many competitors had already come to grief and been captured in various stages of disarray by the world's photographers, who were now massed on the landing side.

Because the bank was crumbling, Princess Anne had been advised at the last minute to jump the fence in a different way from that which she had decided when walking the course. Accordingly, she changed her plan.

'Quite simply, I got it wrong, putting in two and a half strides instead of two or three. Goodwill almost made it, nevertheless; I think he thought he had, but his back toes, which were tucked right under him, caught the pole and he pitched straight onto his nose.' The

Princess, who remained in the saddle until the ultimate moment, hit the rock-hard ground on her right side, jarring her collar-bone momentarily out of its socket. As one of her legs had gone numb from the hip downwards, she decided to retire. With the further experience she now possesses, she says that never again will she alter her original plan of attack.

Princess Anne was looking forward to the 1975 European Championship at Luhmühlen because she now really knew Goodwill and was ready to have a go. The dressage proved easier than she had dared hope for Goodwill. There was less of an arena atmosphere, with the crowd on one side only, and he produced a much better test than normal.

Her round across country came early, at 9.30 a.m. A heavy cold served to blunt her feeling until news of Janet Hodgson's two falls brought her round with a sudden snap.

Goodwill gave her a magnificent ride and she attributes to herself the blame for the sole uncomfortable-looking moment, over the water complex: 'I thought he was going to stand off as he went in and make a big splash; but he had far more sense than I did and had no intention of doing any such thing, slipping in another one and leaving me looking a right charlie, hanging out of the back, while he jumped it perfectly well.'

The course suited the combination admirably, with plenty of opportunities for Goodwill to use his scope, power and athleticism to advantage and make up time. They finished galloping strongly with the gelding pulling like a train as he passed the finish, coming up from 8th to 2nd place. Course-builder Mickey Brinckmann's solid and interesting showjumping obstacles provided no

Intent on the task in hand, Princess Anne and Goodwill clear the 4th fence of the Burghley World Championship in 1974, on the way to 5th place.

60

problems and a confident round completed a magnificent performance, leaving the pair assured runners-up to Lucinda Prior-Palmer and Be Fair, and having made no mean contribution to Britain's team 2nd place behind Russia.

The resilience demanded of world-class riders to withstand disappointing reversals was all too clearly demonstrated at the 1976 Olympics, where, after a heavy fall at the 19th fence, Princess Anne was placed 24th overall, and the British team was eliminated after two horses went lame.

By the next Olympics Goodwill will be 15 years old. Accordingly, his next remaining challenge – which should prove the best ride ever for this superb Royal combination – will be over the rolling Blue Grass country of Kentucky, where the 1978 World Championship will be held.

The trio that won the team silver medal for Great Britain – the gold going to the USSR – at the European Championship, Luhmühlen, in September 1975: from L to R Lucinda Prior-Palmer on Be Fair, Princess Anne on Goodwill, and Sue Hatherly on Harley.

Nelson Pessoa

Born 16th December 1935, in Rio de Janeiro, Nelson ('Neco') was taught to ride at the age of eight by his father, a real-estate agent. Nelson followed his father into the property business, but became increasingly involved in the local riding club's showjumping contests. In 1956, he took the final place in the Brazilian Olympic team for Stockholm, and five years later moved to Geneva, where he built up a very successful string of South American horses, notably Gran Geste and Espartaco. So successful was he, indeed, that in 1965 the Fédération Equestre Internationale (FEI) – governing body of the world's equestrian sport – prohibited riders from competing abroad unless they first spent 30 (later 14) days qualifying as residents. It was not a progressive step, and did little to halt the Brazilian, who was already amassing a huge collection of grand-prix victories.

A more sensible later FEI rule limited European Championships to Europeans. This was only to be expected after the American monopoly: Nelson had won the 1966 European title with Gran Geste, after an all-American jump-off in Lucerne with Frank Chapot (San Lucas) and Hugo Arrambide (Chimbote); and Kathy Kusner won the 1967 Ladies' European title on Untouchable.

An amateur until 1974, Nelson paid for the expenses of running a big stable by buying and selling South American-bred jumpers to rival competitors. His best advertisements were his own spectacular wins on these small, brave, athletic horses. For the Mexico Olympics, however, he chose Russian-bred Pass Opp; for Munich, French-bred Nagir. His stable at Chantilly, where he lives with his wife and son, is now a cosmopolitan mixture: Canadian Houdini, German-bred Saphyr, Irish-bred Oakburn, British-bred Mr. Punch and French-bred Ali Baba. Nelson rode for two seasons under the umbrella of Pernod; and in 1976 moved on to the champagne firm of Moët et Chandon.

An astonishingly prolific winner for the stable is Mr. Punch, whom Nelson took over in 1975. Mr. Punch soon learned to perform acrobatics previously undreamed of and proceeded vigorously to stir up the indoor winter-show circuit. With a magnificent disregard for the proprieties, Nelson now signs on the unassuming Mr. Punch under whatever Moët prefix suits the occasion. 'Today, Moët et Chandon,' he says cheerfully. 'Tomorrow, back to Mr. Punch – who knows?'

This outstanding Brazilian has been at the top of international showjumping in Europe for more than 16 years. A graceful stylist closely allied to the classical American school, Nelson Pessoa concentrates on making all his horses 'bascule' (bend their backs as if following the shape of a hump-backed bridge) over their fences. He has, understandably, become something of a master magician to other riders: French Ladies' World Champion Janou Tissot is one who has benefited considerably from his influence, and former European champion Anneli Drummond-Hay (Anneli Wücherpfennig), who frequently sought his advice on schooling difficult horses, has also paid tribute to his horsemanship.

Had he not become a rider, Neco Pessoa must still have had a wide choice of career: interpreter for the United Nations (he speaks seven languages); cabaret artist (his after-dinner impersonations are legendary); or perhaps impresario (his charm, inventiveness and social graces are allied to considerable business acumen).

In the showjumping ring, he cuts an elegant figure. Small, neat, dapper and unmistakably a Latin with his olive skin, friendly smile and flashing eyes, he doffs his cap to the jury with a flourish, then treats spectators to an exhibition of smooth, polished horsemanship that is a delight to watch. Yet the Latin temperament that makes him so popular has sometimes proved a serious drawback. A great disappointment to him was the outcome of the 1967 European Championship at Rotterdam when, well in the lead with Gran Geste after the three qualifying events, he could do no better than 15th place in the final and so dropped to overall 4th. The strain of trying to keep calm and relaxed during the nerve-racking rest day, when his rivals could go off fishing with nothing to lose, was too much. As

David Broome, who won the title from him, explains: 'It is far easier to come from behind, as I did on that final day, than to maintain a lead over several days, then wait, and do it again to win.'

A grand-prix and jumping-derby specialist, Nelson has been unlucky in four Olympic Games and has forfeited the chance of a medal by turning professional: 'It was the only honest thing to do when Prince Philip (President of the FEI) brought in the amateur/professional ruling.' But it was the quest for those very prestigious medals that brought him to Europe 20 years ago; and he remembers the experience vividly.

'My first trip to Aachen? That is one to remember. I was 19 when I came to Europe with the Brazilian team for the Olympic Games at Stockholm in 1956, and after the Games we went on to Aachen. We were not well known, just a funny team of Brazilians on little horses and we dropped on the Germans like a little bomb. There was Renaldo Ferreira on Bibelot, Eloy de Menezes on Bigua and myself on the grey Relincho (not the one Ted Williams rode later who was also South American, but the prototype).

'The course they built for the Nations Cup would not look big any more today, but then, and especially to us, it looked enormous. We took on everybody at Aachen, it seemed like the whole world and it nearly was: there were twenty-two teams. And these two fellows and myself won the Nations Cup! We shook the Germans so much they counted the scores again to make sure there was no mistake. We thought we were very good to win then, but I tell you, this one that thinks he is the best, he is wrong.'

After that successful 1956 European tour, which included a visit to London and other major capitals where the Brazilian team continued to finish well in Nations Cups, Nelson returned home to Rio, but realized he could not remain there if he wished to continue in top-level competition. 'I knew I could do nothing while I was based at home because we were just too far from everywhere. So in 1961, I finally decided to settle in Europe – first in Switzerland and then in France.'

By the time of the Tokyo Olympics, Pessoa had become one of Europe's most influential riders. He had already won the Hamburg Jumping Derby twice and the British Derby at Hickstead once, and was becoming something of a grand-prix specialist. Not surprisingly, he went to Japan as one of those few tipped to take the gold medal.

'It was the Tokyo Olympics that provided one of my most dramatic moments. I remember it all too well. Gran Geste did not feel very well, and so I jumped Huipil instead. Huipil, who was South American-bred, was very good for me to ride; something like the horses I had jumped at home in the early days. I was competing at Tokyo as an individual, without the Brazilian team, but as the Individual and the Grand Prix des Nations were run concurrently, there was only one showjumping event at the finalé to the Games. In the first round Huipil had a fault at the wall. It was a curious sequence, because the horse hit one block, but it was another that fell, and the jury thought it was not a fault as the other half of the block was still there. We had two other fences down, so the commentator announced 8 faults for my first round. But by the afternoon, at the start of the second round, they had corrected it to 12 faults.

'What happened then was that five minutes before I went in to the arena, I was in the practice ring having a last jump, and Huipil fell over the last fence and crashed down on to my right leg, injuring the knee. The bridle broke, and there we were, both in pieces and going into the ring in minutes. I was hot and cold. I could not feel anything; afterwards I could not walk at all. It was desperate, so I staggered over to the railings where a groom was standing with somebody else's horse, and borrowed his bridle without the owner's permission, just like that.

'I went into the ring in a daze, but it was not so bad as I thought, and we only had 4 faults coming into the last fence. But we were jumping on the athletics ground, and the surface was bad where they had been playing football games. It wasn't the right place to stage showjumping; but this happens so often at an Olympics. Huipil hit the last fence, giving us a total of 8 for the round, and 20 faults overall. We finished equal 5th, and that final mistake meant that we missed the jump-off for the bronze medal by one fence. I know I would have had to have an injection before a jump-off. My knee was very bad; I could not have stayed in the saddle over those fences as it was.'

Just before Tokyo, Nelson had won the Aachen Grand Prix, with Gran Geste; and eight years later during the build-up to the Munich Olympics he won this Grand Prix, run over one of the toughest courses in the world, for the second time, with Nagir. He describes that momentous July day in 1972, tense with pre-Olympic hopes and quarrels:

'This is another one for me, to remember. On the day of a grand prix you put your foot on chance. Sometimes, you know you are going to win; you know the horse and you feel it. I think top riders know their chances, how the horse is reacting to the course, how it fits him. I don't think it is really important for a rider to believe he will always win. I know that over every course I jump, I try to place myself and

Cardiff Castle, Wales, in June 1975 is the backdrop to Ali Baba and Nelson Pessoa during the third leg of the Benson and Hedges Professional Championship.

Anneli Drummond-Hay is on Xanthos in Geneva during November 1969. She had six wins, four of them outright.

the horse against the others. I had two good clean rounds with Nagir that day, but Hans (Winkler) has this problem with his Olympic selection committee, and he rode for his life. I thought we would have to jump off, but then Torphy had a $\frac{1}{4}$ time fault added to his second clear round. We were the only two out in front, and the noise of the crowd, after the time fault was finally announced, was very loud, for Hans as much as for me.

'I have been jumping in Europe without interruption from 1961 to 1977, and have won a lot of national grand prix in France; altogether about 150. Say 45 with Gran Geste,

whom I rode for eight years with no stop; about 25 with Huipil, 25 or 30 with Nagir; but Aachen 1972 was one of the big ones I remember best, when everything went right. Nowadays, it is more difficult to win: better people, bigger combination fences. One thing is, I cannot plan too much before I jump – I have to improve and improvise during the round.

'I would not like to say who is the best

Monsieur Pernod and Nelson Pessoa during the Men's World Championship at Hickstead, Sussex, in July 1974. They finished 17th.

68

rider. Every rider has different moments of success if he fights from March to November. David Broome is very good, but there are about 10 or 12 at the top. Compare riding with race-car drivers. Riding, you think for the horse; you decide when you would like the horse to turn and then there is the fence to judge and the relation between your speed and the fence. You must turn one stride longer or one stride shorter; you must judge. You must decide on the spot, unlike a race-car driver, who must plan ahead or be killed; one mile (per hour) more or one mile less, he dies.

'At school, I played football, basketball, volleyball, ping-pong, swimming. I played with everything a bit – I'm not a stiff leg.' Nobody could ever accuse Neco Pessoa of that.

Gran Geste and Nelson Pessoa descend the Derby Bank at Hickstead, Sussex, in 1965, on the way to winning the British Jumping Derby.

Harvey Smith

Born on 29th December 1938, younger son of a Yorkshire building contractor, Harvey sat his first horse – a Shetland pony – at the age of seven, under the watchful eye of his brother. The 1947 Bingley Show was the scene of Harvey's first competitive jumping (on a milk-round pony), and at 13 he made his début in the show ring with Lady Opal, a near-thoroughbred he had successfully broken and schooled himself. In 1953, in partnership, he bought his first horse, Rose Marie; a year later, he bought the four-year-old Irish-bred bay, Farmer's Boy, who soon fulfilled the promise Harvey had recognized in the ring at Botterill's Sales in York: the pair divided 1st prize in the Open class at the 1954 Barnsley Show with Jim Cowen and Flanagan.

Harvey competed in his first indoor show at Haringey in 1955; but his father died that year, and Harvey then had to go back to building with the family firm. It was 1958 before, wearing a tweed jacket and a determined expression, he reached the Royal International Horse Show at the White City, where, with Farmer's Boy, he won the Young Riders Championship, finished 5th in the King George V Gold Cup and was selected for the British team at Dublin.

The battle of wills has often been in evidence between Harvey and his horses. Warpaint, bought at Leicester in 1961, was one 'difficult' showjumper that in Harvey's capable hands became a big winner. In 1962, he was asked to ride O'Malley for Mr. Robert Hanson; and, with Warpaint and another 'problem horse', Sea Hawk, Harvey soon built up a formidable string on the international circuit. In 1963, with O'Malley, he was 3rd in the European Championship. Another famous horse joined the Smith entourage in that year: Mr. Bert Cleminson's 17-hh Harvester, who with O'Malley shared victory in the Washington puissance on the 1967 North American circuit. Harvester was leading horse of the show and Harvey leading international rider; while in Toronto, O'Malley set a new Canadian indoor puissance record of 7 ft 3 in.

Madison Time dominated 1968 for Harvey; but the great future promised by the horse's performance in the Mexico Olympics was not to be. At the 1969 Royal Windsor Show, Madison Time collapsed and died as he crossed the finishing line, after jumping a clear round. Olympic, world and European titles proved consistently elusive; but in 1970, with Mattie Brown, Harvey Smith achieved every showjumper's ambition: to win the coveted King George V Gold Cup.

In 1972, Harvey turned professional; and further demonstrated his versatility and enterprise by taking up (with notable success) all-in wrestling in 1974, and singing (with a first record, 'True Love') in 1975. But his first love remains the horse. His most recent string has been Johnny Walker, Salvador, Volvo, Speakeasy and Daily Express Foxhunter champion Olympic Star. Sons Robert and Stephen, under the guidance of Harvey's wife, Irene, have become prolific winners on the junior circuit, Robert already having taken over Volvo from his father; so it seems quite safe to predict that the Smiths will be part of the showjumping scene for some years to come.

To Harvey Smith, winning has always been a matter of extreme importance. Indeed, the desperate urgency that so characterizes his every round against the clock is a compelling factor in attracting the crowd to this wild, burly figure. His early reputation, as a tough Yorkshire bricklayer with square jaw, earthy language and rebellious attitude to the Establishment, was well founded on confrontations with the showjumping authorities; though despite several stewards' enquiries and colourful press controversy, he has only been fined once and suspended once. An intensely dominant horseman, Harvey's leap to world fame was aided by the sheer force of his personality. He asks of his horses feats that other riders deem impossible – to Harvey, of course, there is no such word. No matter how many times a gamble fails to come off, his faith remains unshaken: this time, it will work.

There was a time, though, when he felt obliged to say bluntly to his Chef d'Equipe, who was pleading for a fast round in the Aga Khan Cup in Dublin 19 years ago: 'T'old hoss won't be hustled.' Subsequent members of Harvey's showjumping string, however, have been a great deal faster over their fences than was 't'old hoss', Farmer's Boy. The most famous – and perhaps the most astonishing – was Mattie Brown, who Harvey bought in Ireland as Peggy's Pride and promptly renamed: first Condor, then Doncella and finally Mattie Brown. This versatile little liver chestnut, limited in scope but ready to tackle anything, took Harvey to the high point in his career: the moment when he had the rest of the world at his mercy – and nearly won the World Championship.

The drama was enacted at La Baule, on the west coast of France, in 1970: a vast, unfamiliar arena, with the hot, July sun beating down on thousands of empty seats. But there was no one missing from the ranks of competitors, who comprised a fearsome array of the world's very best. Against reigning Olympic champion Bill Steinkraus, Olympic gold-medallists Hans Günther Winkler and Raimondo d'Inzeo, and grand prix specialist Alwin Schockemöhle, what chance did Harvey Smith and David Broome stand, mounted as they were on two apparently unlikely and unsuitable horses?

To add to Mattie Brown's inherent disadvantages (a definite lack of scope which meant an inability to stretch over a combination of big parallel spreads), he had gone lame a fortnight earlier, from an old splint that had flared up again, and Harvey was paddling him in the sea at La Baule in an effort to keep him sound. David Broome, in theory a strong contender, was without his European championship partner, Mister Softee, and had teamed up with the erratic Beethoven, who could (as Harvey puts it) 'beat the best in the world one day – and get eliminated the next'.

Fully aware of Mattie Brown's limitations, Harvey nevertheless knew he had a very good speed horse; and this knowledge was a morale booster with which to attack the first of the three qualifiers, a speed class over a big course. 'Mattie Brown was not bothered by the size of the fences,' Harvey recalls. 'In fact, he went so fast that, despite putting a foot in the water (a fault which put extra seconds on my time), he was still ahead of the field by half a second to win.' The great favourites for the title, Alwin Schockemöhle and Donald Rex, finished 2nd and David, who had started the afternoon badly with terrible after-lunch stomach ache, backed him up close behind in 3rd place on Beethoven.

'Well, that was a good start but I think it surprised quite a few people. I hadn't thought anything of my chances when I went in, and I knew there was still a very long way to go until the final. But an unexpected winner on the first day of a major championship, like that, can make everybody a bit unsure of themselves and of the outcome, especially after a big build-up in the press beforehand. As it was, David and I had got a hold now and we were determined not to let go.'

The second qualifier followed the next day, and it was a puissance. Unlike the usual type of puissance at any international show, when the winner is decided after several jumps-off, over a 7-foot wall, this one lasted for two rounds and Mattie Brown shared 1st place with Graziano Mancinelli on Fidux and Hugo Arrambide on Adagio.

'Surprisingly, Donald Rex, who really was a specialist at these vast, solid fences, hit the parallel in the second round and so that didn't help Alwin's points. David's chances took a knock, too, when Beethoven had one of the parallels down in the first round and they dropped back at the end of the day to 7th place. It left a lot for David to do with a horse like Beethoven, who was so unpredictable.

'But my equal 1st kept me clearly ahead on points, and although I knew that the third qualifier would be Mattie Brown's hardest, my lead gave me a margin for error and this took some of the pressure off. My horse's problem was that, lacking a bit in scope, he could jump big, single fences like those in the puissance but could get into trouble in the wide combination fences in the Nations Cup-type final qualifier of two identical rounds. As it turned out, Mattie Brown made a mistake in each round, once at the combination and once at the big parallel spread towards the end of the course, and took 7th in the qualifier; but we were still

Harvey Smith and O'Malley straining every muscle at Toronto in 1967 – they left with the results-sheet showing a Canadian indoor puissance record of 7 ft 3 in from this jump.

74

well enough ahead overall to lead the other three finalists into the last day by two points. Mancinelli, with only one fence down in two rounds, was 4th in that competition, and overall 2nd, while David excelled himself by winning with the only double clear round. Perhaps the thought that I was certain to be in the final, and he could be left out in the cold, woke him up a bit, because between the two of us it's always a fight to win. So his victory put Beethoven overall 3rd, and then Alwin, who had also had two fences down, like myself, to share 7th, came into overall 4th and last place.

'Now came one of the hardest bits of all – two days of waiting before the strange final, when we were all to ride our own horses, and then, in turn, each other's. Those two rest days made it quite a long wait, but it's difficult to remember exactly what I did. I know I went to the beach, and I know I watched every class in the show; I didn't miss. We weren't allowed to take part; we just had to sit, and that made it hard. I remember seeing Hideaway win that Grand Prix in pouring rain, one of the few things he has ever won. There must have been some pressure, but I don't remember being particularly bothered by the thought of riding the other three horses, not that much. If I had done something drastic – like getting in such a state that I beat my wife, or something – I should remember all about it; but I don't, so it can't have been all that bad. I think probably the worst bit was sitting watching the riders who were out of the Championship back into other classes again, and not being able to do anything about it. You have to keep busy to avoid pressure.

'You can always see when pressure affects other people. Anybody can have a fence or two down, but if the pressure gets to them, then they have a whole lot – seven or eight down. For example, I think this was Mick Saywell's

trouble at Aachen in the 1971 European Championship. He was trying so hard to do well in the first qualifier, the speed class, and that wouldn't be Hideaway's strong point, not in that heavy going. But I know Hideaway, and if the rider feels pressurized and puts that pressure onto him, then the horse crumples and goes to pieces. Some horses will do just the opposite and really try all the harder but Hideaway likes things to be nice and quiet.

'In the early days, I think I used to feel the pressure more; I was always trying to prove myself. If something went wrong in the ring, I usually had to blame it back on myself. If you analyse the reason for the mistakes, it's only occasionally that the horses are not trying.

'Nelson Pessoa is another who has had trouble with pressure. There was the time in Rotterdam when he was leading for the European title, and then fell to pieces and David and I finished 1st and 2nd in the final, while Neco was out of the picture. It happened to him again, in a Nations Cup in Rome, when he could have a fence down and still win; but instead everything went wrong and he finished with a mass of faults.

'About the championship formula: it's not right to run it that way. I might be a bit biased as it finished my chances and David gained by it, but it was a pity. The other thing was that it was all so extraordinary. A fortnight before the event, David and I thought we had no chance at all – Mattie Brown and Beethoven were going so badly, just diabolical – and there we both were, right in at the finish. And this is where I think the formula should be changed. With three good qualifying competitions like speed, puissance and Nations Cup, the decision shouldn't be worked out on a gimmick at the

Olympic Star (Harvey Smith) jumping in The Sunday Times Cup in October 1975; the venue – the Horse of the Year Show at Wembley, London.

Large crowds watched Hideaway, here with Michael Saywell in the saddle, jumping at the Great Yorkshire Show, Harrogate (1972).

end. The trouble is, the horses get progressively more tired as the four riders take it in turns to change. You ride your own first, but this advantage actually worked against me, when Mattie Brown hit the vertical poles and our 4 faults became 5 with the extra 25% added as a handicap for riding your own horse.

'After that, the horses face a biggish track with strange riders for three more rounds and could go on to a jump-off if anyone is equal on points, which happened at Hickstead in 1974

Hickstead, Sussex, in 1975 and the Harvey Smith/Salvador partnership is in action during the Prince of Wales Cup (Nations Cup) meeting in July.

with Eddie Macken and Hartwig Steenken. Those four horses were all wiped out by that final. Look at them – Frank Chapot's Main Spring, Hugo Simon's Lavendel, Pele, then ridden by Eddie Macken, and Hartwig Steenken's Simona. Class horses, but it got right to the bottom of them and took their guts out.

'The competition that sounds the same but is completely different is the Martell Championship every January at Harwood Hall

79

in Essex. It is run on World Championship final rules but the difference is that all the riders are competing on completely strange horses from the start. If it was possible to incorporate that idea into the World Championship final, then that might really decide who was the best rider. Perhaps have the four finalists do their four rounds each on four Grade A horses borrowed for the occasion, and then finish up with a deciding round on their own horses.

'Another thing about the type of final they had at La Baule is that the system is open to attack by a rider who wants to make his horse difficult for the man following him to ride. He could put on a different bit or bridle, stir the horse up by wearing spurs if he didn't usually, or just generally stir him up before handing him over. These, of course, could be tricky things to do and a rider could end up by being too clever if it all misfired and he collected faults on his own horse himself. From my point of view, I was unluckiest of the finalists because I followed Mancinelli on Fidux, and he had not helped me at all by waking the horse up a bit towards the end of his round.

'Fidux was a great big old clonking horse, and I think Mancinelli had been to some trouble to make things more difficult for the rest by altering martingales, loosening curb chains and all that, and the horse was so strong you needed a winch to stop him. There was nothing I could do but try and use my hands and legs to keep going in the right direction, but even so he carted me right into the wings of one fence off the course. Eventually, we ended up with 4 faults, which gave me a total of 9 faults so far, and this did not look too good to me, as the other three riders had been clear on their own horses at the start, while I had not. Another thing was that we did not carry through to the final the points we accumulated in the qualifiers, and so my fight to stay in the

lead was wasted. We all began again from scratch after the two-day rest, and the advantage I had gained over three days – and needed in the final when things were against me – was no longer there.'

Each rider was allowed three minutes in a cordoned-off area in the main ring to get to know the new horse, and he could jump two fences only once. 'It was when I got onto Donald Rex in the third round that everything suddenly came right for me. A wonderful horse, and he fitted me to a tee. Alwin had trained him to do exactly as he was asked: check, and he was there; shorten a stride and it was no problem. He sailed over every fence and felt superb, completely living up to his reputation as one of the world's top horses. Anneli Drummond-Hay told me later that when I rode him, I looked as happy as a king, and it was true.'

But, sadly, Harvey's dream was short-lived. By the time he rode Donald Rex, his chances for the title had gone. David was still on zero after clears on Mattie Brown and Fidux, Mancinelli was clear on Donald Rex but collected 4 at the water with Beethoven, and only Alwin was slipping back behind Harvey with 4 on Beethoven at the water, followed by 8 with Mattie Brown. In fact, Harvey had $^3/_4$ of a time fault with Donald Rex, but it was not decisive. For Alwin, the sadness was that his skill had made Donald Rex into such a good horse that everybody could ride him and he finished up with the best horse's score of $4^3/_4$ faults.

'In the final round, Mancinelli rode Mattie Brown, and although he even tried to imitate me by talking to him in broad Yorkshire, the little horse did not like his style

Hickstead, Sussex, in 1970 and 1971 saw the British Jumping Derby won by Harvey Smith on Mattie Brown, here descending the Bank. It was at the 1970 meeting that Alwin Schockemöhle had two falls with Donald Rex.

of riding and had 4 faults at the water. David could now afford a fence down and still win, but still he very nearly lost it, I think because he thought Donald Rex was easy and he could relax. They wrong-strided into the treble, clouted the first part, then brought down the last. But they were clear over the remainder, and won by a 4-fault margin. Mancinelli took the silver medal with 8 faults, I came in for the bronze after 4 faults with Beethoven, who gave me a good ride, and Alwin was 4th with 16 faults, after a final 4 with Fidux.

'Did the result upset me? There was a time when it mattered desperately. The shock of losing the title, when I had been so close to winning, hit me far harder than I had ever imagined it could do before the beginning. I think this was because I went in thinking I had no chance at all. Even when I won on the first day, I knew I must not count my chickens too soon. But then I went ahead, and I really thought I could win. I thought the final would be a fight-out between David and me, but it didn't happen that way.

'That World Championship was a good experience, because David and I went in, with no hope at all, took our jackets off, said "let's get stuck in" — and came out trumps. Look at all the nations taking part, and still Britain managed to have two there in the final! But for me, it was the same story at La Baule that has followed me right through the big championships and the Olympics as well. In European championships, I have been 2nd twice and 3rd once, and in the Olympics less lucky; but too late, now that I am professional, to have another go at those. And I am sorry to say I think the Olympic Games are false. Too strange a picnic. They are the most talked about, and the most over-rated. There is no bloody prize money, they cost a fortune, and the money spent on staging them and training a

team to go there, could have built the biggest and best equestrian centre in the world. If you do compete, to have a chance you need a team of winners.'

Harvey always remembers with intense disappointment that at the Mexico Olympics the British team was in the gold-medal position '... and then lost everything with Stroller's fall in the second half. And at Munich we were all set to take the team bronze until five minutes before the close. But the World Championship was a more personal matter and losing it, when I had felt the title had my handwriting on it, really upset me when it happened.

'Now it's different. The challenge and determination to win are still there as much as ever, but going abroad constantly as I do, always exposed to this, that and the other pressure of major competition — it stops me caring quite so deeply when I lose. Repetition dulls the hurt. And I think another thing that has helped is my wrestling. Having another interest, another source of income, takes the full-time pressure off showjumping and helps me to relax again and to enjoy entertaining people as I used to years ago as a boy, with a performing sheepdog called Lassie.

'It sounds a far cry from what I am doing now, but I think that showjumpers as well as wrestlers are in the entertainment business. They put on a show for the public. I used to love taking my black-and-white Yorkshire sheepdog, who was something of a freak, to give demonstrations at sheepdog trials. I even teamed up with a fellow who had a performing group of dogs called Athelford's Alsations and a motorbike team called Cytrex, and on Coronation Day, only a year before I bought my first showjumper, Farmer's Boy, I was

Salvador, with Harvey, in the Crawford's Scotch Whisky Championship during the Ingliston Royal Highland Show, Scotland (June 1974).

giving a performance with Lassie and the Athelford dogs at a gala-cum-fête at Wellingborough. As in showjumping, the whole purpose and fun of working with animals is to get them to enjoy the training – while obeying you. And the challenge of taking on a rogue horse and re-making it. Just say it's all about making winners, *that's* the important thing.'

Mio Mio and Dr. Hugo Arrambide (Argentina) found success in 1972 – in Rome, again in Aachen, and here at the CSIO meeting in Lucerne (June).

Michael Matz

The riding career of Michael Matz, who was born in January 1951, began when he was 15. In Shillington, Pennsylvania, where the family then lived, he was offered a ride on a track horse owned by a friend of his father; and Mike was quick to grasp that opportunity.

It proved a wholly enjoyable experience, and he was soon to be observed up at the stables, cutting grass and doing other odd jobs to ensure future rides. Indeed, he jumped at every riding offer or chance. He went trail-riding, even though he did not rate it as 'real' riding; and he joined the Pony Club, which enabled him to ride occasionally at the small local shows, until he reached his 18th birthday and so became ineligible for junior-class competition.

A year later, however, his fortunes took an upward turn when he placed himself in the hands of professional trainer Jerry Baker. Mike first hit the headlines in 1972, when he won the Cleveland Grand Prix with Rosie Report. He won the North American Championship at Detroit in 1973; and membership of the USET squad followed in autumn of the same year. Like fellow-American rider Rodney Jenkins, Mike was to experience the excitement of having his first Nations Cup turn out to be a winning ride.

He is as much at home riding hunters as he is riding showjumpers; and, happily, both approaches satisfy the 'approved' USET style demanded by coach Bert de Nemethy. Mike was a member of the 1975 US team that took the gold medal in the Mexico City Pan-American Games; and in the individual competition there, he took the bronze medal with Grande. He is now the lucky rider of what is probably the most expensive showjumping horse in the world: Jet Run.

When Mike Matz celebrated his 27th birthday in January 1978, he had already won a Pan-American gold team medal, a Pan-American individual bronze, ridden in the Olympic Games (as a member of the US team that was placed in the Montreal Prix des Nations) and won two of the most prestigious events on the 1977 national circuit: the American Jumping Derby and the Philadelphia Gold Cup. And, with Mr. F. Eugene Dixon Jr's magnificent stable of horses – and trainer Jerry Baker – behind him, Mike should be able to look forward to an even brighter future. He has come an amazingly long way in the 12 years since he first rode a horse.

After that first ride, on a track horse at the age of 15, Mike had ridden whenever, wherever and whatever he could; but it proved a less than satisfactory training programme for one who longed to become a showjumper. After graduating from high school, however, he went to work in professional Bernie Traurig's stables and in return was allowed to ride three horses each night. 'But, as one of these was too young to do much, one wasn't quite good enough and one not completely sound, after six months, I decided there was no future for me there.' The experience gained there, however, was to prove invaluable. Bernie, one of the few professionals to have been chosen to ride for USET, was very skilled in bringing young horses to the top; in fact, Jet Run, who Mike was to partner in late 1977, was being shown in national classes by Bernie when bought by the Senderos family.

Mike's next move was to scrape up enough money to buy his own horse, but: 'I could only afford a fox-hunting horse and that couldn't take me far in showjumping, which was what I had decided I wanted to do.'

Vince Dougan, a professional from Westchester, Pennsylvania, gave a helping hand by getting Mike a job with a girl showjumper who, as payment for general grooming, gave him some horses to ride. Then, Vince got hurt on the Florida circuit and asked Mike to ride his horses until he was fit again. One of the first major shows to which he took them was Devon County Show in Pennsylvania, at which, after watching him ride throughout the week, professional trainer Jerry Baker came and introduced himself and asked Mike if he would like to ride for him.

'I was flattered to be asked and pleased to have the opportunity, but undecided for some time as to whether to accept because I thought his place in Ohio, where I would have to go and live, was too far away from both my family and the main showjumping circuit.

'Fortunately for me, Jerry was very persuasive, saying, "If you come with me you'll never regret it" – because although I didn't realize it at the time, it was eventually to prove the chance of a lifetime and lead to the opportunity to ride some of the world's best horses.

'So, in 1970, I went west to Ohio. Most of the horses belonged to Mr. J. Basil Ward. There was really only one top-class jumper, Mighty Ruler, who, like the great racehorse Secretariat, is by the stallion Bold Ruler. There was also a grey hunter called Snow Flurry. We decided he had above-average jumping ability and succeeded in turning him into a jumper good enough to place on the Fall circuit in 1973.'

Mike made his European début as a USET member on the team's 1974 visit, and gained further experience on subsequent North American Fall circuits.

'From the beginning, Jerry and I had got along really well together, and by this time we had become partners, with the major aim of winning gold medals at the Pan-Am and Olympic Games. We work very much as a

team; he doesn't say, "You must do something this way," but rather we work things out together. I feel the way a horse goes – and though Jerry helps from the ground, he rode, too, so he understands this sense of feel and he can see things go wrong of which I may not be aware on the horse's back.'

About four years ago, they moved to millionaire F. Eugene Dixon Jr's farm, near Philadelphia. Mr. Dixon is a great philanthropist: he holds a great many appointments and takes a prominent rôle in promoting art in the City of Philadelphia. His interest had extended to sport (he is chairman of the Philadelphia Sixers basketball team) before he became a showjumping patron, and when his daughter, Ellen, now in her early 20s, became interested in horses, he naturally followed her progress with enthusiasm.

Now that Ellen is primarily directed towards dressage (she has been over to train in Germany), however, her father's interest has turned to building up a stable of showjumpers. In a very short period of time, he established what had become, by 1977, undoubtedly the strongest stable in the US. The catalyst for Mike's eventual move back east, and for foundation of the Dixon-Baker-Matz triumvirate, was Ellen – because, when she wanted to start riding seriously, the person she decided to approach was Jerry Baker.

Although by then (1975), Mike Matz had represented his country in Europe, the United States and Canada, the Pan-Am Games that October gave him his first taste of a major championship. The trip to Mexico City stands out as one of his greatest memories to date.

'When I was told I had been chosen to ride for the US, I felt important for the first time in my life. There is something special about riding

Grande caught at the Aachen grand prix water jump, with Michael Matz.

for a team. My horse was the German-bred Grande. Carl Knee, who trained Michèle McEvoy and is now Chef d'Equipe to the Canadian team, had brought him back from Europe with a group of horses he'd imported. Grande had been bought from Paul Schockemöhle. He was too big and strong a horse to suit Michèle and so the chance soon came to buy him.

'I had been used to riding thoroughbreds, which have a much lighter way of going and found him a very difficult ride at first. He had been brought up to go with his head down and was used to much contact, quite different from my style of jumping. During the first year together, though, we adapted to each other, and now, almost anyone could ride him.

'Going out to Mexico City was a real adventure. My parents came, too, and it was especially exciting to have my father there. He had never flown in an aeroplane before, so it was a real occasion.'

The horses went down to Mexico City immediately after the Philadelphia Gold Cup, five weeks before the Games, in order to become fully acclimatized to the high altitude. 'We exercised them in the mornings and then were free in the afternoons. It gave us a chance to get to know Mexico City and the surrounding area. I had become friendly with Mexican rider Fernando Senderos, whose father had bought the exceptional American thoroughbred Jet Run. We went quite often to the racetrack, and the time spent waiting for the championship passed quickly.'

'The temperatures were quite different from home, because we were so high. It was cool in the early mornings and evenings and really hot during the day, so we went swimming quite often. We stayed at the Jockey Club, which was about 18 miles out of the city, half-an-hour's drive to the Campo Marte

Stadium, which was set in an extensive polo field, where the Olympic jumping was held and the individual Pan-Am Championship.

'The courses set for the Nations Cup of the Games were colourful and well built, very similar to those at home. I recall we all worried about a big, square, natural wood oxer and thought it would be a real problem, but it rode well. But there was another oxer with three discs on each standard (upright) which only two riders were to succeed in clearing – myself and Canada's Michel Vaillancourt. This particular jump had the rail between the top circles, which made it appear far bigger and more imposing than it really was.'

The Prix des Nations, decided in front of 125,000 people in the strangely shaped Aztec Stadium, proved a real cliffhanger. The US team, hot favourites to win the title, had to survive an intensely anti-American atmosphere; they endured a barrage of boos every time they entered the ring.

'Buddy (Brown) was our last rider with Sandsablaze, and in the second round we had to pull for him harder than ever before – that's how it is, being on a team. The Mexicans, inspired by Fernando Senderos, who had registered an outstanding 4, 0, on Jet Run, pushed us to the brink of defeat. Now Buddy could afford only one mistake if we were to win the gold medals.'

Sitting with fellow team-members Dennis Murphy (Do Right) and Joe Fargis (Caesar), Mike held his breath as Buddy landed in the water, an error that was heralded by disturbing cheers from the the Mexican supporters. But Buddy kept his head, and cleared the final light-railed parallels to give victory to the US by the nerve-racking margin of $2^1/_4$ points. Mike says: 'I felt very proud just to be part of that day.'
At the Campo Marte Stadium, where the

individual medals were to be decided, the hard grass surface posed a problem for riders. Only two of the 23 competitors for the individual Grand Prix were clear initially. Fernando Senderos, 22 years old at the time, took the gold medal with just 4 faults in the jump-off with Jet Run, to Buddy Brown's 8 on Sandsablaze.

'Suddenly, I found myself opening a five-horse barrage for the individual bronze medal,' Mike recalls. 'Grande's front legs came over well clear as we took a small wall early in the course on a diagonal, but a hindleg just tapped a block and it swung right out and hit the ground with a resounding crash. There, I thought, went my chance, as I pushed on and recorded a fast 4 faults.

'To my utter astonishment, none of the other four riders, who comprised Norma Meiers for Canada, Mexico's Carlos Aguirre, my own team-mate Dennis Murphy and one of the Argentinians, was able to better Grande's standard. Carlos Aguirre's round on the lop-eared Consejero was by far the worst for me to watch. He elected to go for a slow and steady clear and looked absolutely set to get it until the last fence fell to the ground. To date, I've only stood on the rostrum once – to receive that bronze at the Mexico City Pan-Am Games – but the feeling is sensational, and I hope I'll be lucky enough to get another shot at some of the other major championships. Form changes so fast in this sport. The right horse is absolutely vital, as is luck – you can never be certain you'll even take part, until you've reached the ring and the bell rings for you to start your round.'

But Mike has a better chance than most US riders of making the 1980 Olympics, because he already has the first essential – the

Pan-American gold medallist Fernando Senderos (Mexico) on Jet Run, with – left – Hendrik Snoek (West Germany) on Gaylord, after the pair had taken 2nd and 1st place respectively in the Embassy Masters competition at Hickstead, Sussex.

right horses – in Mr. Dixon's Erdenheim Farm Stables, at Lafayette Hill, Pennsylvania. Also, his riding has greatly improved since the Pan-Am Games, having gradually matured during the two subsequent seasons, 1976 (during which he was a member of the US team who finished 4th in the Montreal Olympics) and 1977.

Grande was 12 years old in 1977 and so still well in line for further Nations Cup and grand prix rounds. Erdenheim horses include Sandor, who won a grand prix in Florida and is considered by many US experts to have Olympic potential. Foaled in 1969, he is thoroughbred by Amber Morn out of the French mare Claire H, and has been brought on very quietly and carefully for two successive seasons.

During the summer of 1977, Mike and Jerry Baker made a brief visit to Europe, ending at the Hickstead International Meeting in July. They jumped Grande and took along Sandor for experience, while Melanie Smith and Fernando Senderos travelled with them.

Jet Run was stabled at Erdenheim Farm at this time. Though he managed to fly up occasionally to ride him, Fernando Senderos had married earlier in the year, was trying to take a more active role in his father's business, and began to realize that he was just not able to devote sufficient time to a horse as good as Jet run. Returning home to Mexico City in August 1977, Fernando decided he owed it to his family to concentrate on the family business interests. In the early 70s, his two brothers had been killed when their private plane crashed and he was now the sole surviving son, who would one day inherit his father's vast and diverse business empire.

In England, Grande and Michael Matz put in the fastest time in the jump-off for the Embassy Kings Stakes, Hickstead (1977) but collected 8 faults.

In early September, he called Jerry and Mike and asked if Mr. Dixon would be interested in buying Jet Run. On the telephone from Mexico City, Fernando told Mike: 'I want you to ride the horse. He is happy at the Erdenheim Farm; I'm an amateur, and it means a lot to me that he has the right home.'

A deal was completed and Jet Run changed hands for a sum which has not been disclosed but is reputed to be a world record, in the region of $250,000.

The Philadelphia Gold Cup is held each September in the JFK Stadium, inside the vast Spectrum Sports Complex, just five minutes from downtown Philadelphia. The turf is good and not chewed up because the stadium is not used very frequently, but, Mike says, 'When a horse comes in the first time, he must be brave or he may back off from the first daunting experience of entering the huge stadium, which holds 110,000 people. After completing the initial round, the horses usually go better and better as they get more relaxed inside.'

'Robert Jolicoeur (who helped build at the Montreal Games) had set a tight Gold Cup course that included two big oxers; but Grande came through with a faultless round in the final jump-off to beat Bernie Traurig and The Cardinal by half a second. I'd never managed higher than 2nd in this competition before.'

Mike reflected: 'To make the win even better, Mr. Dixon, who seldom has time to watch his horses jump, was there. He comes so rarely that it's especially good to win when he does. We had also chosen the occasion to announce Mighty Ruler's retiral, signalling the end of one phase of my career as a showjumper; and now we were also able to announce Mighty Ruler's retiral, signalling the end of one phase of my career as a showjumper; and now, we were also able to ever in national jumping.'

The 1977 Philadelphia Gold Cup carried the second biggest stake money in the States, with $9,000 first prize. The Rhode Island Jumping Derby, also held in September, was the most valuable, with a $12,000 first prize.

The Jumping Derby was founded in 1976, by former Horse Trials rider Mason Phelps, who had represented the US on several occasions in Great Britain in the early 70s. He has created permanent jumps and a course very similar to the Hamburg and Hickstead Derbys, on part of his grandfather's estate at Portsmouth, near Newport, Rhode Island. Olympic rider Frank Chapot was course-builder for the first two Derbys.

Newport is the home of the America's Cup Yacht Race and a fashionable holiday-home area studded with huge mansions that served as a background for the Crosby-Grace Kelly-Sinatra movie 'High Society'. Something of this social atmosphere pervades the ring, which is the biggest in the United States.

'We chose the Derby for my first major public ride on Jet Run. While it was a great thrill to have the chance to ride this superb jumper, it wasn't at all straightforward. When you sit on his back, you get the feeling that, for him, it's all easy. If I ask him to take off too far away, it's no problem, he can lengthen just like that; if I come in a shade close, he'll snap up and contract to help. He has astonishing scope and athleticism.' As Mike is over 6 ft tall and so needs a big horse, another of Jet Run's advantages is that this bay gelding by Jet Traffic stands 17-hh.

'When I first rode him, at Cleveland, we didn't get on so well. Although he'd been in our stables, on the few occasions I'd exercised him, I'd been careful to try and ride him the

In West Germany, Aachen saw the jumping skills of Sandor and Michael Matz, in the June 1976 Internationalen Spielcasinos Bad Aachen.

way Fernando did – which is a very different style from mine – so as not to upset or change him. Fernando had had no time for extensive showjumping training.

'Now, I found him long and strung out; and sometimes, I'd be going round corners with his head pointing the wrong way. Little things can annoy him and it's hard to keep his attention. I don't parade him now before a Nations Cup for this reason. I find he usually loses concentration after five minutes work on the flat. It's quite a problem: this morning, for example, in the arena at Madison Square Garden, where we only have a limited period of exercise time, he gave most of his attention to a little noise in the roof!

'On the first day of the Derby Meeting, he was so strong in the collecting ring, he was almost running away with me. Jerry, who was watching us, realized this and came and said, with disbelief in his voice: "Michael, *this* is Jet Run!" And I felt helpless as I answered: "I know, but what can I do about it?"'

What Mike did about it was to go out and win the American Derby. Jet Run produced the only clear out of 30 rounds on going made difficult by an earlier deluge of rain.

Many of the permanent Derby jumps are named after the European counterparts on which they were modelled. The Vichy Double Banks, which were first used in Vichy, France, are twin banks with facing vertical sides. Pulvermann's Grob was designed at Hamburg by the German rider Pulvermann for the first Derby ever held; he was later killed, trying to ride it. It is a three-effort Sunken Road-type complex and the basis of the Devil's Dyke at Hickstead.

Mike remembers: 'While it was wonderful to win, it didn't give me such a lift as the Gold Cup because I couldn't help feeling I was rather lucky, so early on in our partnership. Jet Run took a very good look through Pulvermann's Grob but still jumped it pretty well. The Bank rises through three tiers, to a height of 9 ft, and is based on the one at Hickstead, although it is not so high. There is enough room on top and it rides about the same. At the bottom, there are about three strides to vertical white poles. Jet Run almost stopped at the top, then crept into what felt like space. The only thing I was worrying about was not to look for the distance until he landed at the bottom; maybe three strides, if we were close in, or two good strides if further out.'

The USET of which Mike and Jet Run were members won all three top international team honours and captured two out of three Nations Cups on the 1977 North American Fall circuit of Washington, New York and Toronto. At the final show, Toronto's Royal Winter Fair, Mike was leading rider and won the Grand Prix with Jet Run.

This success provided a magnificent ending to 1977 for a rider whose biggest victories must surely lie in the future.

Debbie Johnsey

Debbie Johnsey, the eldest of four children, was born in July 1957. A neighbour of the Broome family, near Chepstow, she was the youngest rider in the equestrian events at the 1976 Olympic Games, where in the Individual showjumping she took 4th place on Moxy. She was no stranger to being the baby of a team: she had been selected to take part in the 1969 Junior European Championship, riding her pony Champ V, when she had not yet reached her twelfth birthday. After a German journalist had pointed out the FEI rule which states that riders must be at least 14, however, Debbie was withdrawn from the Dinard team.

Two years later, she was in the junior team at Hickstead, where she finished 11th in the individual classification, and had one clear round in the team contest. No British team went to the European Championship in Cork in 1972; but at Antwerp, in the following year, Debbie won the individual title on Speculator (who shared the sire of Grand National winner Specify). In the 1974 championship, because Speculator was unsound, she rode Assam, a seven-year-old American-bred ex-racehorse bought in New York by her father. They went into the water in the first round; but the pair nevertheless helped the British team into 2nd place.

Since her senior debut at Rotterdam, in August 1975, there has been no stopping Debbie Johnsey. With her father's coaching, she jumped herself onto the British short-list for Montreal as a result of two grand-prix victories in Europe; and then proceeded to jump herself into the Olympic team, having collected the Amateur Championship at Cardiff on the way.

In the time since the Montreal Olympics, Debbie has continued to show top-class form at home and abroad. She helped the British team to win the Nations Cup competitions in Paris and Geneva, and was selected for the British European Championship team of 1977.

Overleaf, Debbie with the first foal of Champ V. Champ played a large part in the early stages of Debbie's riding career, and is still ridden by her younger sister, Claire.

The coming together of Debbie Johnsey and Moxy was a miraculous affair for British showjumping. It happened chiefly because Terry Johnsey, a former National Hunt steeplechase jockey, spotted a bay thoroughbred competing in small jumping classes in the North, followed a strong hunch, and bought him fairly inexpensively in July 1975. At that stage, the 11-year-old Tarbet did not seem to be much of a bargain: though his breeding was impeccable, he had gone through the Doncaster sale ring at least twice as a cast-out from racing. It was something of a Black Beauty story: before joining the Johnsey family, Tarbet had clearly seen a very unhappy and seamy side of life.

Debbie formed a sympathetic partnership with the new horse from the start. She rechristened him Moxy – Jewish for guts and courage – and a fresh chapter for both of them began. After only a month's acquaintanceship, they joined the British team for the Rotterdam show and impressed colleagues with some exceptionally promising performances.

It was not until the following March (a bare four months before Montreal), however, when Debbie won the Grand Prix of Dortmund (albeit on another horse, Croupier) against fierce continental opposition, that the Olympic selectors added her name to the short-list. But on a pre-Olympic tour of Germany and Switzerland in May, Debbie and Moxy jumped clear rounds in the Aachen and Lucerne Nations Cups and virtually selected themselves. The only worry remaining was that of pressure on a relatively very inexperienced girl of just 19. As Chef d'Equipe Ronnie Massarella pointed out: 'It would be a different matter if Debbie could be the one young member of the team, supported by, say, David Broome and Harvey Smith. That way the pressure would be off her and on to the

older riders, who would be expected, rather than hoped, to go well. But as it is, Debbie and Moxy are the only permanent partnership of the whole Olympic showjumping contingent and they will be expected to be the stars. It is asking an awful lot.'

Ronnie was absolutely right: Debbie was really out on her own. And this is how she remembers it: 'The first round in the Individual Grand Prix was the biggest I had ever jumped. The first fence was a big parallel – nothing like at home where you often have a small brush to get you going. You were in there jumping for your life from the start. Then No. 2, a green and white upright after a left turn; then No. 3, a big parallel oxer, very wide. You turned right-handed past the ring entrance up the wide perimeter fence to No. 4, an enormous upright with very awkward striding towards it.

'The fifth fence was a rustic double and the start of where your horse needed Olympic scope. Both parts were silver birch poles over water, and the first was a parallel over a ditch, then a difficult distance, then another parallel oxer, over water, a fraction bigger. After that you turned right across the ring to No. 6, an upright rails over a balustrade and back again on a small loop to No. 7, a wall oxer, then a sharp left-hand turn to the water, No. 8. And this was where Moxy made his only mistake.

'You went across the ring then, to another upright, then a right-hand turn to an oxer over a viaduct wall, No. 10; then you turned at right-angles to rails over a water ditch with a big spread. Then you veered slightly left to a big wall and turned again on half a circle to a huge triple with a spread of over 7 ft – No. 13, where Peter Robeson and Law Court had their 4 faults.

'Straight on from the triple you ran on to

No. 14, an enormous treble at the side of the ring. This was a parallel followed by one very long stride to another parallel; and they were both very, very wide. The last part was an upright and you needed to meet it dead right or you couldn't get out. Then you turned right-handed to the last, an absolutely enormous oxer, and that was the end of the first round. If only Moxy hadn't had the water!

'The second round was massive. It started off with a big wall, then an even bigger upright, then two enormous parallels, and then No. 5, a double of rustic uprights that only seven out of the 20 horses in the second round jumped. Then came No. 6, a very big parallel, followed by an awkward striding into the water, and here Moxy landed fractionally short again. Then came another enormous parallel that you could have driven an old double decker bus between, then an upright, and then that huge silver birch treble. Moxy tried very hard and nearly made it, but the upright in the middle made a horse steady up after stretching over the triple, and then they could drop short for the last spread.'

But Debbie's total of 12 faults for the two rounds put her right up at the front of the field, with the Canadian Michel Vaillancourt on Branch County. Two from the end, they were joined by Belgian François Mathy on Gai Luron. Alwin Schockemöhle was left, but it seemed impossible to imagine the superbly in-form Warwick doing much wrong. And, indeed, he never gave a single chance, to record a double clear round and take the gold medal. But Debbie faced a fight in the jump-off, and in appalling weather conditions. Minutes after Schockemöhle had confirmed his victory, the heavens opened. Thunder and forked lightning rolled round the hills and torrential rain transformed the sandy arena surface into a lake.

Moxy is the mount for Debbie Johnsey at Lucerne in May 1976; she was one of only two riders to have a clear round in the Nations Cup.

The jump-off was postponed until the storm abated, then Vaillancourt, well supported by his home crowd, went first of the three medal contestants. Unperturbed by the wash he put up, Branch County was round for only 4 faults, in a fast 29.8 seconds.

But Moxy had not reacted nearly as calmly as Branch County to the nerve-racking delay, and to the drenching rain. Debbie shudders at the memory: 'I had Moxy ready for the jump-off but then it was postponed – he got very upset by the wait and went off the boil. When I came out into the ring to jump, the going was very deep. I think cantering over the water scared him – Moxy will jump in deep going, but not in water – and then he hit the first fence (very unlike him) and that upset him, too.

'That double of uprights in the centre of the ring, No. 5 in the second round, was where Moxy got into trouble. He hit the orange poles going in, stopped at the second part, and there was no way he could have made it from where he landed between the two elements. And I knew then and there that the medal had gone. Did I feel the pressure? Once through the start, one's mind is oblivious. But afterwards, when the medal had gone, my heart felt as if it was falling right out. I wanted to go out and buy a tin medal for Moxy – he had been so marvellous.'

Moxy's score of $15^1/_4$ faults was nowhere near as fearsome a figure as some of the earlier totals had been, and British spectators held their breath when Gai Luron also faulted into the double; but the Belgian pair still eased comfortably into the bronze-medal place.

'The pity was that the time allowance was not tighter,' says Debbie. 'Moxy can go fast, and I had always been told, particularly by David and Harvey, that time is vital at the Olympics; that almost everyone has time faults. Moxy was well inside the allowance each time, except in the jump-off when he had a stop, but some of the others were much slower and only just made it without time faults. Had the time been quicker, as everyone said it should have been, it would have suited me better. And I might not have had to jump off against François Mathy, who I think was only just inside the time.' Without a jump-off, of course, Debbie would have been assured, at least, of a bronze medal.

David Broome comments here: 'It would be wrong to make an excuse out of the time allowance, but what I think the coursebuilder did was not to measure the course tight enough. It is certainly true that Olympic times are usually desperately tight. I did notice in the team event at Montreal that people were wasting time all over the place and still not getting time faults, so Debbie really has a point there.'

Debbie has happier memories of another

dramatic finish: the 1973 Junior European Championship at Antwerp. 'There were four of us left for the second jump-off against the clock. I was first to go on Speculator, who went very fast but put a foot in the water.' Debbie's time of 33.6 seconds was quite enough to frighten the other three riders into trying very hard indeed. 'The one I feared most out of the other three was Stany (van Paesschen, from Belgium); but Smart Alec faulted at the water, too, and Stany finished nearly 5 seconds slower, to be runner-up, with Norbert Koof (Germany) 3rd in 39.1 seconds. It was a really nice title to win.

'But going to Montreal and finishing 4th was special. The Olympics, they were always my ambition. And Moxy proved good enough to go there. He should go down in history as one of the great horses – he's an athlete.'

Hickstead, Sussex, was the venue for the Nations Cup event in April 1976, where Debbie Johnsey rode Speculator.

Graham Fletcher

Born 9th January 1951, eldest of three children of a North Yorkshire hunting farmer, Graham was educated at Thirsk Grammar School. His sister, Elizabeth, is married to David Broome. A member of the Bedale Hunt branch of the Pony Club, Graham competed in junior classes; his main interest then, however, was football, which he still enjoys as a spectator.

Having learnt the basics of showjumping with inexpensive ponies, notably Crispin (with whom he qualified twice for Wembley), Graham progressed to sound, half-bred horses, most of them bought by his father for very little money and shaped by his own determination into top-class international performers. He first caught the notice of Olympic selectors at the 1970 Bath and West Show, on Buttevant Boy and Joe Pullen's Talk of the North. A month later, he won his England Cap at Aachen, and initiated an impressive run of Nations Cup performances over that most testing of courses. The 1974 Rome Nations Cup, too, saw a brilliant display of horsemanship when he jumped an 8-fault round and a clear on a completely strange horse (Malcolm Pyrah's Law Court) over a big course.

The lady who insensitively demanded of Graham in Rome that year: 'Why have the British sent a second-rate team?' could well have shaken the confidence of a lesser man; but Graham is possessed of that famous Yorkshire grit. It was the same quality that sustained him through 1976, after he injured his right shoulder and upper arm in a crashing fall at Hickstead. Normally a cheerful, outgoing character, Graham became desperately depressed when told by doctors he had no chance of getting fit for the Olympics. But the Middlesborough Football Club's physiotherapist came to the rescue and, encouraged by Chef d'Equipe Ronnie Massarella (who swore he would get Graham to Canada, even if by stretcher!), Graham rapidly improved and his selection for Bromont was confirmed. He felt, however, that Double Brandy, having missed out on European competition in May and June, lacked the experience essential for Olympic fences; and neither Buttevant Boy nor Tauna Dora (owned by Mr. Norman Burrows) had the necessary scope. In the event, Graham rode Trevor Banks's Hideaway, but the horse was only half-fit and the partnership was not a success.

Moscow should be a happier story: with the right horse, a rider of Graham Fletcher's skill must have an excellent chance of bringing home a medal.

Aachen, that gruelling West German horse show (whose fences are said to be the most massive in Europe, if not in the entire world), is a favourite training ground for teams wanting to test their potential Olympic strength. The Americans are regular visitors before each Games, and even the Japanese have made forays there. For the British, however, trying out an amateur Nations Cup team, Aachen 1975 turned out to be an unparalleled disaster – and a brilliant success. The paradox arises from the startlingly different results of team and individual competitions.

Rowland Fernyhough, the talented Welsh amateur, hit the headlines first by finishing a most creditable runner-up on Autumatic to Alwin Schockemöhle and Warwick in the three-leg German Championship. Then came the Nations Cup, in which the British team had hoped to put up a good showing against the seemingly invincible home side. In fact, they exceeded their expectations by taking the half-time lead, and really had the opposition struggling. But then the Germans rallied and equalled on points to force a jump-off; and only now did the foe really show its teeth, as Graham Fletcher recalls:

'When we took the Germans to a jump-off in that Nations Cup, in the last round they put the fences up very, very big to suit those German tanks of horses – I think the course went to the biggest I've ever seen. The parallels were moved out, the distances were changed – everything to do us in; and that didn't leave a very good taste in our mouths.' The treble combination had become a double; but the spreads of the obstacles and the distances between them were sufficiently extended to exclude all but the horse of immense scope, the genuine Olympian. It was all too much for the neat, scissor style of Tony Newbery's Warwick III (already applauded for a

memorable double clear): he stretched once, over the first double, hated it – and dug in his toes for good at the second.

The path to glory had become the path to despair. Rowland Fernyhough's Autumatic had two refusals and many faults; and although Graham's Buttevant Boy, with a 4-fault total for two rounds earlier, floundered bravely round with two fences down, there was no situation left for Malcolm Pyrah to save with April Love. 'They really gave us a plastering,' says Graham, ruefully. 'Tony was eliminated, Rowland had refusals and all that, my old boy Buttevant Boy had two down ... It was a good achievement on our part to take them to a jump-off – but you have to concede their achievement, too; although I know everything suited them. Buttevant Boy has always had a lot of character and guts, but he took quite a hammering in that Nations Cup. So to come out two days later and win the Grand Prix was quite something!

'When I walked the Grand Prix course beforehand, I thought that if Buttevant Boy really did all he could, he could go well. But I would never have thought the two of us were going to win. When you see the fences on your feet, you see them through the eyes of your own particular horse, and what kind of mood and form he is in that day. When Buttevant Boy is really firing on all cylinders and really on the ball, he can be much more active and athletic than his rather solid shape suggests. I know exactly what kind of fences will stop him or cause trouble: extra wide parallels and spreads following on from each other in a combination: the sort of thing you expect to meet at the Olympics, and the sort of thing we had faced in the jump-off for the Nations Cup at the Aachen show. It takes real scope for a horse to cope with that, and Buttevant Boy just hasn't got it. That is why I refused to entertain

the idea of taking him to the European
Championships at Munich the month after
Aachen, or to Montreal the next year. It would
have been madness. He would have got
completely buried; he could have turned over
and hurt himself, trying for the impossible.

'The Aachen Grand Prix had two
complete rounds, and then there were four to
go in the first jump-off. The Belgian horse
(Pomme d'Api), ridden by Eric Wauters, went
out with a time fault and myself and Buttevant
Boy were next to go, second. (You'd think a
full-blown course of 17 fences, twice – coming
after a hard week and a gruelling Nations Cup
shoved in – would be enough; but no.)

Tauna Dora (Graham Fletcher) competing in the July 1975
Prince of Wales Cup (Nations Cup) held at Hickstead, Sussex.

'In the second jump-off, everything really
mattered; I was right up against it, and as first
to go, I knew I couldn't waste much time. The
Belgian with his time fault had in fact been a
big help because I knew I couldn't afford to
hang about; but Buttevant Boy is not a speed
merchant, he is a steady-paced jumper. I could
only try to go fast enough to give the others
plenty to do. And the combination, I thought,
was big. They had changed the fences for the

Graham Fletcher and Buttevant Boy at Aachen during July 1973.
On three occasions they have jumped in Nations Cup
competitions at Aachen and gone clear in one of the two rounds.

second jump-off against the clock, and the last two were a very big wall followed by the final fence, a spread oxer. I went as fast as the track would let me, and dared to put the pressure on.

'Alwin Schockemöhle went next on Warwick, and surprised me – and probably everyone – by having a brick down from that huge wall. Warwick is, after all, a fantastically powerful horse who can jump those kind of fences for fun, but perhaps his judgment went wrong just at that moment when Alwin was pushing him on. Then came Hendrik Snoek on Rasputin, who somehow seemed more threatening than Alwin. Rasputin was jumping extremely accurately (he is anyway faster than my horse), and coming to the last fence Snoek was up on the clock. I got really tensed up – I knew that we could get beat.

A consistent partnership at the Horse of the Year Show and the Courvoisier Championship at Wembley, London in 1972 – Germany's Hendrick Snoek on Faustus.

'But, suddenly, it was the Dublin Grand Prix all over again. That was 1971 and the Grand Prix jump-off: I had already done my best on Buttevant Boy, but Hendrik and Faustus could certainly beat my time if they went clear. Curiously enough, it was exactly the same situation then: he was up on the clock coming to the last fence – a double, one part of which was a gate – coming across the ring towards the jury box. And just when he had it all in his pocket, Faustus sent the gate crashing down.

'Now, at Aachen, Hendrik boobed again, doing just the same thing. I am not sure whether Rasputin got on a wrong stride, whether he was pushed along too fast or whether he went at the fence right and simply dropped a foot on it. My impression is that it may have been the pressure of knowing that he had to go faster than me, and also clear, that preyed on Snoek's mind and made him just that bit careless. Anyway, Rasputin hit a pole on the spread, and brought it down to groans of dismay from the German crowd.' Thus the Aachen Grand Prix came to Britain, for only the second time since the Second World War.

'Preparing for a competition like the Grand Prix of Aachen demands a certain ritual, if you like. And I suppose I have got used to doing this mental preparation, this thinking, on my own. The only time I get any outside help is in the collecting ring, just before I jump; Miles, my groom, acts as groundsman and tells me how the horse is going. My father, who always comes with me to shows, keeps well out of the way before I go in to the ring. For me, it is no good doing a lot of talking, or asking endless advice. I have to school myself to tackle it alone because when it comes to it, in the ring, you and the horse are out there on your own, and *you* have to make the decisions, be wrapped up in what you're doing.

'I won't say that much about the Olympics, but I will explain the difference. There, at Bromont, I was not my own master,

Graham Fletcher partners Clare Glen during the Olympia, London, Show in December 1974.

because I was riding Trevor Banks's horse, and he wanted to govern the preparation. He planned it all, and so I never really got involved, so I could never get tensed up as I usually do, as I *need* to do to produce my best. I have always run my own show, whereas at Bromont, I was the supporting cast for someone else. It felt strange, and I was never so wrapped up in that Individual Grand Prix, and the ability of Hideaway to cope with the course. I am used to the horse being my responsibility; I have learnt to stand or fall by that.

'But Aachen, that was a day to remember, in a week to remember. I have had some good wins since I joined the international circuit in 1969–70, but until I won that Aachen Grand Prix, my best moment had been the Dublin Grand Prix four years earlier. What made it all the better was that I have been in the British team for Aachen regularly since I started international showjumping in 1970, and winning there has always been a nearly impossible dream. There was the incredible contrast between the disastrous end to the Friday's Nations Cup – the terrible, depressing, final knowledge of defeat on rather a grand scale – and then, right on top two days later, on the Sunday: the enjoyment of defeating a really first-class field! No flukes, no concessions – though certainly luck because one always needs that – but, simply, being the only one to jump four consecutive clear rounds on that day. That was involvement with the task, right up to the hilt.'

David Broome

Born in Cardiff on St. David's Day (1st March), 1940, David McPherson Broome is the eldest of four children, two boys and two girls, who have all made a success of showjumping. His father, Fred Broome senior, is widely recognized as one of the most knowledgeable horsemen in the country; before an eye injury in a hunting accident in 1976, he was always responsible for the groundwork of David's horses. The family now lives at Mount Ballan Manor, Crick, near Chepstow, where the house and farm look across to the romantic medieval Castle of Caldicot.

David started riding Shetland ponies about the time he learned to walk, and by the age of nine was a veteran of the local pony shows and the hunting field; Biddy, Beauty, Coffee, Chocolate, Ballan So-So and Ballan Lad were his partners in these early campaigns. At 16, he competed for the first time in the showjumping classes at Badminton, coming 2nd to Paul Oliver. The next year, 1957, his father paid £60 for the big bay 10-year-old Wildfire, an army reject who became leading money-winner in Britain with David in 1959.

In 1960, David made a tremendous international impact by taking the individual bronze medal on Mr. Oliver Anderson's chestnut, Sunsalve, at the Rome Olympics, and then the World Championship bronze at Venice. The King George V Gold Cup at the Royal International Horse Show, London, followed and in 1961 the partnership won the Men's European title at Aachen. But Sunsalve died in 1962, and until he teamed up with the Massarellas' Mister Softee in 1965, David travelled the show circuit successfully with Ballan Silver Knight, the Argentinian Olympic horse Discutido,

and the brilliant mare Bess. But he had to borrow Jacopo from his brother-in-law, Ted Edgar, to ride in the 1964 Tokyo Olympics. With Mister Softee, however, David formed a legendary partnership, winning such prizes as the King George V Gold Cup, two more European titles, another Olympic bronze medal and the British Jumping Derby at Hickstead. For the 1970 World Championship at La Baule, David put up an inspired performance to win on Mr. Douglas Bunn's wilful but able gelding, Beethoven, but rode Mr. Cecil Attwood's Manhattan in the 1972 Munich Olympics.

In 1973, David turned professional, riding four horses leased to the Esso Petroleum Company, but the 12-month contract was not renewed because of the oil crisis. Esso horses Sportsman and Heatwave formed the basis of David's string shortly afterwards, when he joined forces with Phil Harris under the sponsorship of Harris Carpets (now Harris Acrilan Carpets); star performer, however, became the American thoroughbred Philco, bred from similar blood lines to Triple Crown winner Nijinsky.

An intrepid traveller, David has competed three times on the North American circuit, once in California and regularly on the indoor winter European circuit. He lives at Mount Ballan Manor with his wife, Elizabeth (Graham Fletcher's sister); helps to run the Wales and West showjumping meetings held at the farm three times a year in a Hickstead-type outdoor arena complete with Derby Bank; and is also Joint Master (until 1977, with his father) of the Curre Foxhounds, hunting whenever showjumping permits. Other hobbies are shooting and golf.

David Broome once admitted that if he had not taken up showjumping he would have liked to become a racing driver. And, plainly, he has the temperament – cool and apparently nerveless – for such a sport. The vehicle he drives most these days, however, is a ten-ton truck. In this horse transport of delight, he seems happy to drive for thousands of miles across Britain and Europe, sometimes catching a cross-channel ferry by night and jumping the following day. It is a fatiguing pattern of existence, and one that many of his international opponents would shun. Yet for David, who possesses a great deal more stamina than one might at first suppose, it is an accepted way of life, a means to an end.

But let no-one imagine that this pleasant, amiable-looking driver in the old clothes who has just rumbled casually into the horse-box park, will be casual in the ring. It is there, as horseman *par excellence* with sensitive hands and the most brilliant sense of timing in the business, that he stands out so remarkably above the rest.

'Sitting on the grass with Harvey (Smith) at the Royal Highland a fortnight before the 1970 World Championship, we thought the whole thing was going to be a disaster. Then we got to La Baule, and we walked the course for the first day. It was meant to be a speed course, but it looked bigger than a grand prix, and we thought "God help us in the days to come". I remember thinking how all the other riders had freshly clean jackets and breeches, and there were the two of us, not quite so elegantly turned out. But 85% of them were no good, and that gave us fresh hope.

'I was pleased because Harvey won the class on the first day. The puissance was very big: Beethoven had a fence down, and Harvey won again. Then I knew that the chips were up against it for the last qualifier. I was placed 7th,

and I had to do something. I went all out absolutely determined to win – I had to. Harvey upset me, I think; he was so cockahoop about being in the lead that I was needled into pulling out something extra. And from that moment on, when I won on the last qualifying day, Nations Cup day, to pull up to 4th place – there was a different feeling for me, in my attitude to the whole thing, and I sensed also a different feeling amongst the other riders.

'I think, to be honest, the thought of riding Beethoven didn't exactly appeal to them, and I don't blame them. For me, I was at least the regular rider of Beethoven so it was not so bad, but they had all seen the kind of things he could do, when he trotted and bucked into that big treble in the last qualifier. Of the four horses for the final, three were difficult – only Donald Rex was the exception. Mattie Brown, Harvey had converted to an honest character. Fidux was a big thumper, terribly strong and looked awkward. And in the two-day rest before the final, the riders were thinking what they could do to make their own horses difficult for the rest. It was a very long time to wait.

'I think Harvey slept a lot of the time. I was sharing a room with Ted Edgar, my brother-in-law, and he was a great source of inspiration. He talked me into winning, kept telling me it would be easy, that of course I was going to win. It worked wonders. But all the time you were riding the other horses in your mind. The only one I never gave a thought to was Donald Rex, and he was the one who gave me the most trouble, as it turned out. It was unfortunate for Alwin (Schockemöhle); they were all problem horses except for his own – it's not an advantage to be a Christian in that kind of a final!

'There was no thought of any tricks on other riders; I was just determined to go in and do the best I could with Beethoven on the last day. In a final where you all change horses, the system is obviously open for a rider to abuse it by making his own horse extra difficult for someone else, perhaps by revving it up or something like that. I felt that Beethoven was quite enough of a headache on his own without trying to make him worse – honesty *had* to be the best policy. You get nowhere by being too clever; you just get caught up in your own wash. My father warmed up Beethoven on the final day as much as he ever did normally; we took no short cuts.

'But that final-day course made us think a bit. Harvey and I had only had the Martell Championship (the Harewood Hall event run on World Championship lines every January) to prepare us, and that is 3 ft 9 in on strange horses. This was 5 ft 3 in, and it was a bit different!

'I planned it fairly well, I think. I positioned Ted up in the crowd area by the second warm-up place to tell me his opinion of the other horses, and he was marvellous. Absolutely right, every time. Fidux, Graziano Mancinelli's horse, I tried to quieten down. Alwin and I were a bit scared after Harvey got run away with on Fidux. My God, Harvey – he's so strong, he bends nails and tears up telephone directories just to keep fit, so what chance had we got? Well, I thought I'd try the opposite tactics to Harvey, who tried to use his strength to hold him and got nowhere. So I took a long rein, and let him hunt on – it worked like a dream. But I must say in all fairness to Harvey that he had the unenviable task of following Mancinelli on Fidux, and

Ted Edgar in action on the Everest Double Glazing-sponsored Everest Snaffles, at the English Royal Show in July 1972.

Mancinelli had stirred the big horse up like anything over the last fence – the water. Well, this was bound to upset the horse as he was a marvellous water-jumper anyway and he wouldn't expect it. In fact, this business of having the water at the end of the course so impressed Douglas (Bunn) that he put in another fence after the water at the Hickstead World Championship four years later. At La Baule there was too much opportunity for a

Graziano Mancinelli, who brought Fidux to the 1970 Men's World Championship at La Baule to the discomfort of the other finalists, competed on Lydican during the European Amateur Championship at Munich in 1975, three years after winning a gold medal at Munich.

rider to steam up a horse there – but I'm bound to say that I don't think Douglas's effort made a lot of difference – in the end the outcome of both those world championships was decided over the water jump. On an overall view of the whole thing, I don't think horse changes are that great a way of deciding a championship.

'Mattie Brown was another problem horse for me, and it was a big relief once he was behind me. He could have stopped, run out on me, reverted to his old habits, done anything; I didn't know what to expect. Mick Saywell saw Mattie Brown jump the water with me, and he said afterwards that we were so close to landing on the tape that it wasn't true. So I had a bit of luck there; in fact, the two English horses saved both Harvey and me at the water jump – amazing when you come to think of it, when you think of Britain's reputation at the water, always the big bogey.

'But Donald Rex was the one. When it came to my turn with him, the last horse I had to ride, I had 8 faults in hand. And he was a dolly of a horse to ride; I was so complacent about it that Ted told me not to fall asleep! Everything always seemed to work so perfectly when Alwin rode him that I thought I would just sit in the saddle and wait for it all to happen. It never occurred to me that he might not react quite so quickly as I expected. Anyway, we only made the treble because he is a horse with a fair amount of scope. We had eight strides to go, and there I was taking a pull, but nothing happened at all, except that he lost impulsion and seemed to slow down. We couldn't get a good stride by then and Donald Rex hit the first part rather hard, cleared the second part but then had the third part down. I was lucky to get through the treble at all – his scope saved me.

'We then had two fences to go, and there were still 4 faults between Mancinelli and

Philco, with David Broome, is here competing for the 1975 John Player Trophy at the Royal International Horse Show, Wembley, London.

myself. If I had one more down we would have to jump off and that was the last thing I wanted – the horses were tired, and although Beethoven had really behaved extremely well so far, I felt certain his sweet mood would never last if I climbed back and asked him for yet another effort.

'The last-but-one fence was a big upright. I took a big hook at the reins, and Donald Rex jumped it by a foot. Then the last was the water. We took off over it absolutely together and he was six foot in the air over the tape on the far side. What a brilliant horse. I thought: that will do, that's the end.

'But the awful thing was going in to collect the medals. We stood on the rostrum to get those, and then there were more prizes still. Eight of them, and apparently, all for me. It was so embarrassing, they kept coming back for me each time, to give me something else, and nobody else got anything. Douglas gave a party afterwards, that evening, for me, and Ted – imagine it – spent £180 on champagne! All the way through, Ted was such a wonderful support for me; he was so confident that he made me feel the same way.

'I felt a bit sorry for Alwin, though. He was entirely responsible for training Donald Rex into such a super horse, and instead of helping him at the end, it backfired on him. He must have known this and it can't have helped his confidence during the two-day wait. In fact, Alwin and I together watched Harvey ride Fidux and he wasn't going to ride him after that. He thought the horse was really dangerous, and he didn't want to risk his neck. But after I had ridden Fidux, with much happier results, Alwin changed his mind and decided to have a go after all. They got along fairly well.

'Looking back on that World Championship, it was just as well that I didn't have Mister Softee to jump there. It would have been asking far too much of an old horse. At the time, in the spring of 1970, when John Massarella decided not to let Softee go to La Baule, I thought it would all be a disaster. But he was right in the end. Softee had done his bit the year before at Hickstead, when we won the Men's European title from Donald Rex; and it was quite interesting to compare the two horses, whose careers were fairly closely matched from the 1967 European Championship (when Softee won, and Donald Rex was 3rd) until 1970.

'Donald Rex had more scope going down to really big fences, but Mister Softee was just that bit sharper. Hickstead in 1969 was a good example of that: Alwin was in the lead, and Hans (Winkler) and I were sharing 2nd place, but the points were so close that whoever won the last leg also won the title. The rules of the competition suited me, because there was a time and faults aggregate over the two rounds; and Softee was a very, very fast horse. Although it was a very long and big course – 18 fences – for the first round, Softee kept up his flowing rhythm the whole way and finished

The 1974 English Royal Show, at Stoneleigh, Warwickshire, saw David Broome competing on Sportsman.

The legendary Raimondo d'Inzeo, here on Merano, visited England for the Royal International Horse Show in 1961.

clear and fast. Alwin was clear as well, but Donald Rex had been 3 seconds slower, which gave them that much more to do in the second round. On the draw, I went before Alwin, and as long as I didn't blow it, he had to keep up with me, not the other way round. Softee jumped his heart out: pressure jumping at its best – poetry in motion.

'Alwin, of course, with that 3 seconds lost after the first round, had to make up time and that was a hard thing to do over that course. In all fairness to him, Alwin had a right try and by the time he got to the water jump, Donald Rex was nearly 3 seconds up. But the horse was blown, his stride got elongated and there was no way Alwin could get him back in time to

clear the treble. He had two fences down, but one was enough to decide the title.

'At the Mexico Olympics in 1968, Softee was the best horse on an overall average for the Individual and team Grand Prix, with Donald Rex just behind. Softee put up a better performance in the Individual with his bronze medal, but Donald Rex was the best in the team event. We had this very tight time allowance – I think the course-builder must have been a good deal out when he measured the course for the time allowance as there were only four rounds jumped without time faults. Softee had two of them, Raimondo d'Inzeo and Bellevue had

another and Marcel Rozier was the fourth on Quo Vadis. I saw the first two horses jump – with time faults – and I knew I would have to push on very fast and cut the corners. Nobody would disagree that Softee had few equals going against the clock over a big course, yet even he could only get round in the exact time, 98 seconds. In the second round, in the afternoon, I think he was a fraction of a second inside the allowance. Donald Rex, who finished the team event as the best horse, with $18^3/_4$ faults as opposed to Softee's total of 20, had time faults in both rounds. But Alwin knew his own horse, and perhaps if he had pushed Donald Rex, he might have lost his accuracy.

'Well, those were the Mexico Olympics, and the disastrous end for Britain when the gold medal vanished with Stroller's fall. But at least Softee's record there had been reasonably good, even if we did all lose our enthusiasm in the slump from top to bottom.

'Four years later, at Munich, it was just the opposite. Manhattan had gone well in the first round of the Grand Prix des Nations, for 4 faults, and I was the last of the team to jump in the second half. I don't know what went wrong, but the result couldn't have been worse. I was half expecting trouble, because when I went to warm him up for the second round, he had changed into quite a different mood from the morning. Maybe the general excitement of the crowds waving flags and getting ready for the closing ceremony had unsettled him; I don't know. But I couldn't get him to concentrate and when we had two fences down early on, I knew we would be very lucky to get all the way to the end of the course with only one more mistake. As it was, we had 16 faults and it could have been twice that. We could have had three fences down,

Heatwave in action with David Broome in front of large crowds at Hickstead, Sussex, for the Prince of Wales Cup (Nations Cup) in April 1976.

and still won the bronze medal; but they all came down like ninepins, even the last one, and the medal went to Italy. I felt as if I could take Manhattan and myself into a hole in a field and disappear inside it.

'But the extraordinary thing was how that horse can change. After the disaster in the Games on the Monday we went to Rotterdam on the way home – and on the Friday, Manhattan won the test (puissance) in the most fantastic way. He gave the wall a good foot all over! I don't know exactly how high it was, just under 7 ft, I think, but he got the most fabulous stride going down to it. About five strides out, everything was perfect, and everybody watching us knew it was going to be perfect. He took off and exploded over the top of the wall – it was a most marvellous feeling, especially coming after the horrors of Munich. I've been down to that wall ten times since then, and won that test twice again, and I've never got the same perfect stride.

'Tests can go very well or very badly. Manhattan jumped his highest-ever wall in New York in 1973, clearing 7 ft 1 in; but in Rome once, he hesitated before taking off for the wall, and catapulted me off. I hit the ground before he did, and being Rome, it wasn't that soft. It was also a very long way to fall – but I remember lying on the rock-like ground, roaring with laughter. I think Manhattan sort of cracked back as he jumped, and off I shot.'

It is often hard for the spectator to comprehend how horse and rider have the nerve to gallop, apparently fearlessly, towards an obstacle like a 7 ft wall; and even to seem to enjoy it. Occasionally, of course, a horse loses courage at the last moment and ducks out; just as a rider may suddenly waver and experience relief when his mount grinds to a halt. But David Broome has never faded in this way: extreme confidence in his own ability and a cool temperament under fire seem to be the hallmarks of his skill. There are times, however, that even he does not care to remember too often:

'There was a fence at the 1960 Rome Olympics, in the Individual Grand Prix, a fence coming out of the treble that was half a stride out, either way. That was terrifying because anything could have happened, but I thought Sunsalve would be all right – he had the ability to do away with half a stride.' In fact, Sunsalve hit the last element of the treble in the first round, but David said at the time that other riders' doubts about the possibility of only putting in one stride had shaken his own convictions and caused him to ride the treble half-heartedly. His faith in himself and his horse was later justified, for they were well clear at the treble in the second round, still putting in one stride only.

'And then there was a big parallel at the 1964 Tokyo Olympics – you could have parked a London bus between the front and back bars. I looked at that the first time and wanted to go home! But the fence was on its own, and so I thought I had a better chance of jumping it than if it had been, say, in a combination – and, happily, it didn't look quite so bad when I looked at it the second time. I cleared it once in two rounds.'

Well known for his onward-bound style, David nevertheless places much importance on control. Lack of it dismays him. 'I recall going into a double much too fast, when the horse snatched the reins from me. I knew I had to get in control very quickly, or I was for it; but at the last minute, I managed it.'

Alwin Schockemöhle

Alwin Schockemöhle, second son of a farmer who also bred horses, was born in Vechta, North Germany, on 29th May 1937. His international career as a horseman has spanned 22 years, from the Junior European Championship at Rotterdam in 1954, when the German team was 2nd, through to the 1976 Olympic Games, at which he won an individual gold and team silver medal.

At 17, he became a pupil of Hans Winkler at Warendorf; and in the following year, Alwin was almost lost to showjumping: he was in the German team that took part in the 1955 Turin three-day event, and was short-listed for the 1956 Stockholm Olympics as a three-day event rider; though he finally went to Stockholm as reserve rider for both the three-day and the showjumping teams. Thereafter, he concentrated on jumping, riding the horses of Hans Freitag, in whose factory Alwin worked during the day — in the evening, he schooled Freitag's horses. Now, Alwin has his own steel-mesh factories, two in Northern Germany and one on the Ruhr.

He gained a 1960 Olympic team gold medal in Rome, on Ferdl, and a team bronze in Mexico City (1968), on Donald Rex. In world championships, he was not so successful, reaching the final only in 1970 at La Baule, where he finished 4th. As for the Men's European Championship, one German newspaper suggested that for Alwin it was a case of 'always the bridesmaid and never the bride'. At Rome (1963) and at Hickstead (1969 and 1973) he finished 2nd; his temperament, it was suggested, lacked the killer instinct — a theory Alwin must have taken great

delight in disproving at Munich in 1975.

Alwin's easy-going nature, and his essential fairmindedness, have made him popular with colleagues and spectators alike. It was therefore with surprise and sorrow that the showjumping world learnt, on May 4th 1977, of his decision to retire. For over 10 years, he had put up with pain from displaced discs and vertabrae, damaged originally in falls; but the moment of decision came after severe back trouble that began in April 1977 as he started training for the summer season. After treatment, his back improved; but he felt that if he continued to ignore medical advice, he could well end up with crippling spinal damage. He continues to run a first-class stable of showjumpers, ridden by two pupils, and also does some schooling of young horses himself.

The disappearance of this superstar horseman, reigning European and Olympic champion, has deprived European audiences of a much-loved favourite whose challenges in the ring have become legend. It also robbed showjumping of the long-awaited confrontation between Alwin, David Broome and Eddie Macken, the three most brilliant European protagonists of the era, at the 1977 European Championship in Vienna.

Of his momentous resolution, Alwin admitted: 'The first few months will be the hardest. But I have been around a long time — too long, perhaps. Now is the time to go, when I'm still O.K.' So he went, quietly, leaving behind him a standard of skill, courage and sportsmanship that will remain difficult, if not impossible, to follow.

It is impossible to imagine a more deservedly popular Olympic champion than Alwin Schockemöhle: a sportsman to his fingertips. David Broome is one who has great respect for the courage and ability with which Alwin faces up to a challenge; but it was also David who presented Alwin with his toughest-ever assignment, one day in his life that the West German has never forgotten. He recalls: 'The 1969 European Championship at Hickstead, that David won with Mister Softee – I think it was one of the closest championships I ever remember, because on the first day, David won and I was 2nd, on the second day he was 2nd and I shared 1st place; we were always 1st or 2nd. We finished even together with 6 points, after the final; but David took the title because he had the better placing on that last day.

'It was a very hard final. It was against the clock, I remember, and he was very fast with Mister Softee. In the first round he was 3 or 4 seconds ahead, so I had to go. The last section of the course was 33% shorter in the second round. You have the first round in three parts: the speed, the Nations Cup part and the puissance. In the second round, the puissance part is out, so the line is 33% shorter, so I had from then on two-thirds of that way to make up the 3 or 4 seconds faster that David had been in the first round. But it wasn't possible, and I went too fast.

'David says that by the time I got to the water I was about 3 seconds up, and maybe I was, but this speed was so much that it was a risk. David's second round had been fast enough and I had to make the time from the first round because they counted together. I was so fast that it was really not safe. It was the only chance – I had to do it, to take it. I lost it in the first round for sure, because David is not a man who goes slow, not any time and not on

that horse! If you do it with Winkler and Torphy, you could do this even if you are 10 seconds too slow – you can get the 10 seconds back in the second round; but not with David and Mister Softee. I try everything; I tried for the chance but it was too fast.

'In '75, the European Championship again, with Warwick this time, that was a good final but I think it was a little bit more testing and with the crowd at Hickstead, because it was close – David and me together, even to the last rider jumping – who will win nobody knows. But in Munich, I was 2nd the first day, the next day I won equal 1st (with Orlandi and Fiorello) and took the overall lead, and there was only one man who had a chance to beat me, and that was Orlandi. But he took the wrong course, on the last day. So I could make something like 28 faults and still win. There was no pressure. And with Warwick, you see, he was a little bit of an outstanding horse all that summer in Germany. He had won the German Championship, won in Aachen, and he was in super form, and at Munich he was still in super form with very little there to challenge him so he had a really good chance to win. But in 1969 with Softee and Donald Rex, there were two super horses and two riders in form.'

For Alwin, the build-up to the 1976 Olympics in Montreal was fairly frantic: early in the year, Warwick had caught a virus infection and his recovery was slow enough to cancel out any thought of early training. With rivalry for the coveted Olympic team places running fever-high, Alwin's absence inevitably caused gossip on the German national front. The Olympic committee despatched scouts to the Schockemöhle stables to make an official report on the condition of Warwick; and the pressure increased further when he incurred a minor training injury. At Aachen, in late May, there were hurried

consultations in corners; and Alwin looked as if he was fighting with his back to the wall.

It was a curious situation for British aficionados to follow: Britain was searching under stones for a hidden champion to put in her team while Germany, it seemed, was busy hurling them out. World Champion Hartwig Steenken suffered a reversal in one of the qualifications and was dropped, as were two more from the Munich gold-medal quartet, Gerd Wiltfang and Fritz Ligges. Then, just when Alwin looked to be edged out as well, Warwick recovered in time for the final qualifying trials. But even after the announcement of the German Olympic team, rumours of fearsome rows persisted on the issue of Warwick's selection for the Individual Grand Prix.

Alwin must have been vastly relieved to reach the training quarters of Bromont and finally settle down to the job in hand with a fit horse. Warwick had to be the one to beat: everybody on the European equestrian scene knew this was the class combination; but the question that remained for many, was that of Alwin's own temperament under pressure. He had the reputation of being too accident-prone on the big occasion; it was only 11 months earlier that he had won his first-ever European title, an extraordinary plight for a man who had been winning grand prix in Europe for nearly 20 years. Rex the Robber had fallen at the water jump during the 1973 European Championship, and refused three times in the 1974 World Championship; Donald Rex had turned turtle at Hickstead in the jump-off for the British Derby; Wimpel had broken down in the mud at Aachen in the 1971 European Championship; and Alwin himself, outridden

Schockemöhle, '75: with better luck than the previous year, and Warwick, Alwin on the way to clinching the European Amateur Championship individual gold medal at Munich – in action in the third leg of the competition.

by three opponents in the 1970 World Championship at La Baule, had once said despairingly: 'I am unlucky. I shall never win a title; something always goes wrong. Perhaps I shall give up trying – it's no good.'

But those who credited Alwin with over-susceptible nerves were proved gloriously wrong at Bromont. He won the Olympic title, a showjumper's highest accolade, with a record-breaking performance of two clear rounds that had never before been achieved. And he did it in a way that made the rest of the field look very mediocre. No man who cracked under pressure could have stood up so triumphantly to the onslaught of that day.

'That'll teach you all a lesson,' declared 1968 (Mexico) champion Bill Steinkraus, from his place in the press seats where he was running a TV commentary. 'Those of you who thought Alwin had bad nerves ... Look at that performance today – it had everybody else running for help but he never twitched.'

Alwin himself says: 'Bromont was the best thing I ever won; it was the biggest course I ever jumped in my life. I have never jumped a course bigger than this one.

'There had been troubles enough before the Olympics, but they were the politics you always get before a big competition like this. Warwick had a virus infection three months before the Games – just the time I wanted to start training again – and then he was back in training and he injured a leg, and was lame for another ten days, so he was only in training again for a few days before we left for Canada.

'When we got to Canada, there was some doubt about my going in the Individual, because normally in Germany they had three qualifications before the Olympics and Warwick had only jumped in two of them. So there were the politics with the other riders, because some of those riders had tried to get

Warwick out. It's always the same – there is a jealousy if you have won a lot like Warwick had – the European Championship, the German Championship. So there was a lot of feeling at Bromont when I was chosen to go in the Individual and Sönke Sönksen was left out. I think it was the way he was told that made him so upset; it could have been a little bit more tactful.

'I walked the course for the first round at Bromont, and I didn't think that I would be clear, but I knew that I could be. The horse jumped very good in the training at Bromont; from the first day we arrived in Canada, he went better and better, and there was no discussion in the whole team that we shouldn't jump in the Individual later. Officially, the decision was not made until declaration stage but all the riders in the team, and the Chef d'Equipe Gustav Pfordte, knew right from the start of the training that the one horse who would have to jump in the Individual was Warwick.

'I had no problems in the first round. In the second round, the only trouble I had was when he touched one fence – the first pole of one oxer – but not enough to make a fault. Otherwise, he jumped it all easily. That was my good chance, when I saw the course and I thought it was very big but I knew that I had a horse in really top form, and I knew that my horse would be jumping more than 70% or 80% better than all the horses in the competition, so for me it was much easier than for the other riders. I knew he could do it because he can jump water very well, he can jump verticals, or an oxer or a double of oxers and so I knew that he could do everything.

Rex the Robber in 1973, at Aachen, with Alwin Schockemöhle wearing the 'leading rider of the show' armband. On Rex the Robber he won the Grand Prix of Europe (on the occasion of Aachen's 75th year), and the prestige Meisterspringen (masters jumping competition) – entry is limited to reigning champions. He also won two speed classes, on Weiler.

I don't think it would even have been difficult for me if it had been a smaller course with tighter distances; Warwick is a horse who seems to be able to do everything, a speed class one day, a puissance the next and a grand prix the next.

'When it came to the second round, the only thing I was afraid of was the weather; there was a thunderstorm coming, and if my round had been two or three minutes later it would have been very difficult for me. When it rains like that, it gets into the horse's eyes and into his ears and he might not jump so well – they don't like it. So I had very good luck, to just finish my round before the water came down. I don't like riding on bad ground; but for me it was OK, both times when I jumped, not like the other riders had it for the jump-off. This ground became so bad after the storm, but at least it was sand and not so slippery as it would have been on grass or mud, like at Aachen, Cologne or Hickstead.

'When I came in for the second round, it was unnecessary for me to jump clear again, therefore I was very quiet; there was no pressure. I was last to go, and even if I had 12 points (3 down), I would have had to jump off for the gold medal – that would not have been so good. But I told myself that the horse was in good form and the next best score was 12 faults, so I could have two fences down and still win the gold medal. I hoped that I would have no kind of catastrophe, nothing like a wrong distance, or a fall or something more than 12 points. I thought maybe I might have one down, or with a bit of bad luck, two down; but it was unlikely I would have three down. But you can't know; sometimes you do a wrong distance – you arrive at a fence, you see, and then you have a fall and so you have 12 points very easily. It happened to the British team, to Peter (Robeson).

'I was so very pleased that day, all the good things came together. The rider trusted the horse and for a special class like this was, you need that trust. I had that trust with Donald Rex also, but otherwise, to compare my two outstanding horses, Warwick and Donald Rex, that is very difficult. They are rather different horses. You see, for a horse during the season I think Donald Rex was the better horse because he was much more uncomplicated. He was a grand-prix winner every Sunday if you wanted, not like Warwick because Warwick is sometimes not so easy to ride; there can be a little bit of a problem with his mouth and if you prepare him for one class, two classes, that is OK – but you ride every day full speed with him. But on the special courses he is for me maybe better than Donald Rex, or maybe the same – because he jumps everything. He jumps high, and he can go fast and he never stops and that is always a good feeling for a rider. Donald was the same, but Warwick was a little bit more a puissance horse than Donald; a little bit more scope.

'Donald was a wonderful horse. I should always have liked to win a gold medal on him, but he had a little bad luck at Mexico. In the Individual Grand Prix he was not in top form. I think he would have been good enough to win the gold medal there, but he only was on top form for the Nations Cup there and you have to have your horse in top form all the time to win. Maybe the change of food upset him at Mexico; he had not completely acclimatized, I think. If

Peter Robeson on Woodlark during the Fontainebleau Nations Cup in June 1975.

they had run the competition the same way as at Tokyo, with the Individual medals decided together with the team jumping, he would have won the gold medal because he was the best horse. I would like to have made a challenge against Billy Steinkraus, because there was always a chance to beat Snowbound when he had 4 faults in the second round. I think the Individual, except for one oxer which was very big, was not so big at Mexico as at Bromont. Maybe Donald arrived a bit late in Mexico. He was difficult because he was a horse that always had too much blood, and this may have affected him. This is not an excuse, I have no excuses. Sometimes if a rider makes a mistake he is looking for an excuse in the horse. I saw this in the film later on – I made a recording of the Olympic film. I thought it was my fault but I

don't think it was. He made two faults in both rounds, touching the fences at normal speed and the way he did it was not his way.

'But I have been lucky to have two horses like Donald and Warwick, two really good horses. I think, maybe, Donald Rex had the more quality. If everything was right with him, he jumped like a machine. Fantastic in the mouth, to ride, to turn, every direction. One season I started in 15 grand prix and he won all the 15, and that is for any other horse impossible, even Warwick. He was like that against a lot of good horses, like Askan, like Simona; even though Simona was fast in a jump-off, and Donald was behind her, he could

Schockemöhle, '73: stretching out over the water with Rex the Robber at Hickstead, Sussex, during the Men's European Championship. Alwin finished 2nd (14 points) to Paddy McMahon (7^1/$_2$ points).

beat her by two-tenths or by half a second and
that you can't do with Warwick. He is much
more difficult. I suppose I could also say that
buying Warwick was much more difficult,
because Donald Rex had come from Hans
Pracht – the husband of Eva-Maria Pracht, the
dressage rider – but Warwick had had a lot of
owners. When he came to me I don't think he
knew which way to turn, everybody had tried
to teach him something different.

'He was first of all owned by a farmer,
then sold to the brother of Jurgen Ernst near
Verden, then Ernst sold him to Hartwig
Steenken. Hartwig sold him to Leon Melchior
in Holland, then Melchior sold him back to
Hartwig, then Hartwig sold him back to
Melchior, then Melchior sold him to Jurgen
Ernst, and finally – I bought him from Jurgen
Ernst. It's quite a story!'

It took a little time for Warwick, a giant
of a horse and exceptionally headstrong when
Alwin bought him, to come to terms with the
idea of a quiet, controlled approach to his
fences. But Alwin is essentially workmanlike in
the saddle, and a long-time believer in the
value of basic flat work. His grounding in
dressage helps to get the powerful horses he
rides light in hand, hocks beneath them, ready
to take off. The method he uses hinges on this
power-control system, which then explodes
into action a few strides before the obstacle.
Despite a constantly recurring series of back
injuries, Alwin possesses a strong seat and uses
it to great effect as he drives the horse on to take
off precisely on the spot marked X. Alwin's
method was brilliantly put to use with Donald
Rex, but David Broome, who adopts a more
onward-bound and therefore less exact style,
had great trouble discovering which lever to

Schockemöhle, '74: bending low, Alwin on Rex the Robber
before a packed house at the Rotterdam CSIO in August – the
same year that the same mount refused three times in the World
Championship event.

press when jumping the horse in the World Championship final at La Baule.

As well as undisputed riding ability, Alwin has another invaluable asset – he is quite outstanding at spotting a horse's potential. He has had so many showjumpers passing through his stables at one time or another that it is almost easier to list those he never bought rather than those he did. It would be, clearly, quite impossible for Alwin to hold on to all the horses he has tried out, but even so, he distributes them among his rivals with typical generosity, some sold, some – in his own words – 'given to ...' Thus might a property tycoon in a Monopoly game give a helping hand to his opponents by turning a blind eye to the rent.

In private life, too, Alwin is something of a tycoon, with the running of three steel factories that takes up three-quarters of his week. But despite a ferocious work schedule that prevents his competing for the first three months of every year, he is unfailingly courteous – and never too busy or intense to make fun of his latest disaster. One such occasion I remember very clearly, illustrates

this. We shared a plane-ride from Heathrow to Dublin; only a few days earlier, on his way home from Heathrow to Germany, Alwin had had £3,000 in cash stolen from his suitcase. The spoils had been his winnings from Hickstead and Wembley, and were put in a suitcase together with a gold watch for his wife – which was not touched. For a time I tactfully refrained from mentioning what I assumed to be a painful subject; but then I ventured sympathy – to be greeted with howls of mirth and: 'Well, I only hope that whoever took it, had a good night out with a girl afterwards.'

In just the same way did Alwin make light of another disaster; perhaps a more crushing one, in terms of human endeavour. The loss of the 1970 World Championship at La Baule he felt, and measured, in terms of his own failure. He refused to accept commiserations of 'bad luck, finishing fourth'.

'It was not bad luck,' he told me firmly. 'The best man won, and that was David. But there is something for me: when Donald Rex took the points for the best horse out of the four in the final. He was wonderful, my dream horse.'

Lucinda Prior-Palmer

Born in 1953, the daughter of a major-general, Lucinda Prior-Palmer was to make history as the first rider to win the Badminton three-day event with three different horses. She has also made the record book as a result of her victory in the 1975 European Championship, held at Luhmühlen.

Her success began with the arrival of Be Fair, an inexperienced five-year-old bought for her by her mother when Lucinda was just 15. After a season hunting, Be Fair began eventing with Lucinda at Rushall. There was not much to report from that first Wiltshire outing, close to her home on Salisbury Plain, where Lucinda was a member of the local branch of the Pony Club. But the following season saw the two of them improve to make the British team for the Junior European Championship at Wesel, Germany, where the team won and Lucinda was 11th. She then went across the Irish Sea, to Punchestown, and came 4th in her first senior three-day event.

In 1972 she made her first appearance at Badminton, where she was happy to finish 5th; and it came as no surprise to find her in the British team for the European Championship in Kiev in 1973, where the British were defending the title they had won at Burghley two years earlier. She showed some of the family courage (and a wealth of female endurance) by remounting after Be Fair fell at the fifth fence; although in some pain, she continued to the end of the course. Her final placing was 12th.

She had another jolting fall at Badminton in the following spring but nevertheless ran as an individual in that year's World Championship, where her only error was too slow a speed on the steeplechase course, a mistake that cost her five places in the final reckoning. No such mistake was made the following year, however, when she won the European title and took an all-girl team into 2nd place behind the Russians. Later that autumn she won the Dutch three-day event at Boekelo on Wideawake, the horse that would tragically collapse and die the following spring after carrying Lucinda to her second Badminton triumph.

After Be Fair's breakdown on the Bromont cross-country course, this courageous young rider could have been forgiven for contemplating retirement; but she rallied yet again to take second place at Burghley with Killaire. The 1977 season saw even greater triumph: at Badminton, on George (like Killaire, almost a 'chance' ride), she gained the Whitbread Trophy for the third time – and, remarkably, also took 3rd place with Killaire. A week later, she broke her collar-bone in a fall from Hysterical at Locko Park, and it is perhaps typical of Lucinda Prior-Palmer that she was very much more concerned about her horse than about her own injury.

Lucinda Prior-Palmer is a girl whose enthusiasm is matched only by her colossal determination to succeed. For her, 1976 was a year of tragedy – first with Badminton then with the Olympic Games – yet she pulled herself together after the Olympics in a most professional way to ride a new horse into a close finish at another major three-day event only a few weeks later; and by the end of the year, she was writing a well-planned essay on the future of combined training in Britain, underlining the need for harder work, more initiative in the sport, and greater professionalism.

To Lucinda, everything connected with the hard work of eventing is fun; as those who were around one sunny April morning in 1973 at Badminton might recall. Dazzlingly garbed in banana-yellow headscarf, black sweater, yellow skirt, black stockings and patent shoes, she prepared to trot up Be Fair in the veterinary inspection before the judges. Against the background of green/brown tweeds and other comfortable country gear of nondescript hue, this startling apparition stood out like some glamorous wasp. The idea of the colour-scheme, she confided with a huge smile, was to shock the judges into such a state of mental paralysis that they would fail to notice any small irregularities in the action of Be Fair – who could have been a fraction stiff after the cross-country efforts of the previous day that had taken him into the lead.

Lucinda's vital personality is clearly reflected in the pioneering spirit that has led her to work her way across America from east to west, on a package tour to Russia and an expedition to Iran (which included a trip round the Shah's stables).

She has also travelled as a competitor with the British three-day-event team to America, Germany, Russia, Holland and Canada. For help in showjumping, she took herself to the maestro himself, Hans Winkler, and for instruction in the art of dressage, she sought out a colleague of Alwin Schockemöhle; two realistic efforts at improvement that endorse her words in the Midland Bank Horse Trials handbook: 'The ability to enjoy a sport need not be muffled by the desire to perfect its technique.'

Her own quest for this perfection began some years ago with the Junior European Championship team; then came senior competition and, eventually, Badminton – the Mecca of every event rider. At first attempt, Lucinda and Be Fair finished 5th; it was 12 months later, in 1973, that the partnership got away from the rest of the field, to hold a clear lead. The starting point of a brilliant future, it nevertheless had, as Lucinda recalls, a horribly shaky beginning:

'I think the luckiest and the most dramatic moment for me was, without a doubt, the Coffin at Badminton in 1973. It was very early on in the course, the third fence, and Be Fair had not got going at all. Worse still, I was trying to ride him without a martingale, and this didn't help either; in fact, it became a nightmare. He almost stopped, over the first part of the Coffin, a post-and-rails, but somehow, incredibly, he slithered over it. But in so doing, he completely landed with his head facing almost in, opposite the ditch he was supposed to jump with flags in the middle. Instead of facing it, he was facing the ditch – well, well left of the white flags, and by the time I could stop him, he was down in the ditch. And what I did – if you can visualize it, in that deep, dark, horrible ditch – was to turn right and kick along the ditch, along the bottom, until I got him between the flags. Because, unfortunately for me, the flags were on the landing side in the ditch of the Coffin,

not the take-off, and then I pulled the left rein and he had to jump out of the ditch up the bank. He did a sort of shuffle up that vertical bank, and over that very, very stout rail on the top of it, and he did it – I just don't know to this day how.

'For a start, he should have stopped at the first fence, and then we had this terrible time at the Coffin. After that, he began to warm up and move on faster, and things went right for us all the way round the course. The net result was that we won, but he was so incredibly lucky – he wasn't an experienced horse.

'Of course, if he hadn't got over the Coffin, then he would not have won and would not have gone on anywhere else, like the European Championship at Kiev that autumn and so on. So getting through that particular drama really accounted for a lot. It set off a chain of events for both of us. The thing was, Badminton was a very severe course that year, not one to repeat. All the way round, it was endless punishment for the horses; drop after drop, and then you faced banks to climb up and drop down again.'

Lucinda was by no means the only one to have some very anxious moments at that third fence. Of the 69 starters, some 24 incurred penalties at the Coffin for either refusals or falls, and plenty of horses more experienced than Be Fair had an extremely sticky passage through it. The problem was that, with only two obstacles behind them, the horses came through the heavy going on the old turf in the park, made a sharp right turn through an enormous crowd of people and, after only a few strides, came face to face with a forbidding expanse of solid, black poles. If they were brave enough to tackle the 3 ft 6 in rails into the Coffin, they shrank back

Be Fair, with Lucinda Prior-Palmer, taking fence No. 12 in his stride in the cross-country section at Luhmühlen in September 1975.

in alarm from the mysteries of a black, murky dyke below them, a good 4 ft wide. If they somehow survived all this, there was still impulsion to find from somewhere to clamber out over a towering rails of 3 ft 9 in above them.

'After Badminton, we were chosen to go to the European Championship at Kiev; a course that produced some very bad moments. The second fence (on the cross country), the one that caused all the trouble, had an awkward downhill approach, but we drove into it hard and fast to clear the big spread. Be Fair nearly made it, but caught a hind leg as he landed and I was thrown too far forward. Somehow he made a brilliant recovery and regained his balance.'

But despite surviving the horrors of that infamous second fence (which caused 20 falls, 15 eliminations, a host of refusals and some very unpleasant incidents of bloodshed), Lucinda had a fall later in the course, and had to ride on with an injured knee. Her perseverance, however, together with Janet Hodgson's incredible courage, ensured that at least Britain came home with the team bronze.

The next milestone in Be Fair's calendar came at Luhmühlen, 1975, scene of the next European Championship. Lucinda recalls: '1975 was Be Fair's year. In the dressage phase at Luhmühlen, he went like a dream.' At the water, No. 6, riders had two alternatives, with four separate efforts involved. They could take the right-hand side of the artificial lake, over a post and rails and water to drop down and land on a centre island bank, then on again over an upturned punt to the deeper water, splash across and climb out the far side to a sleeper-faced bank followed by another set of rails. The British team favoured this quicker method, but the Germans took the opposite path down the left-hand side. This was a post-and-rails drop over a sleeper bank into the water, then a fearsome-looking jump up to a wooden bridge across the lake, and off again into deeper water over more rails. The exit was over a trellis fence onto the bank. Be Fair took the right-hand method. Lucinda says: 'Everything went right for us; but I was not looking forward much to the Normandy Bank.

'This was a combination of three fences: a brush into a small wood, jumping from sunshine into darkness. Then a check for a sharp left turn over a fallen log at right-angles to the brush. A stride later, we had to find the impulsion to jump up to the top of the Normandy Bank, and be exactly right for the post and rails off the top of it, and the steep drop to the far side.'

There were plenty of defaulters here, with the light-dark-light patches temporarily blinding the eyes and the demanding zig-zag turns at high speed. But Be Fair took up the individual lead after the cross country with almost scornful disdain for the very imposing obstacles, and a clear showjumping round confirmed Lucinda as the new European champion.

Her winning form continued. At Boekelo, the Dutch international three-day event six weeks after Luhmühlen, her second string, Wideawake, galloped through thick fog and some hairy moments on the wooded cross-

Lucinda Prior-Palmer about to jump off the Normandy Bank at Boekelo, with Wideawake in October 1975, having just overtaken Helen Cantillon on Wing Forward, who has just emerged from the fog.

country course to help his rider score yet another European success. And so came Badminton in 1976, the pre-Olympic test that Lucinda, understandably, does not care to recall in its entirety:

'At Badminton, Wideawake suddenly showed how super everything was and I thought then: that horse has just such a fantastic chance. It was absolutely one of those lucky things; he was at 'au point' fitness; he was exactly right to the very day. You just looked at him and thought: "Christ, this could be it!" Once we started on the course, I just felt he had it in him to win, and he went on from fence to fence getting better and better and

better. I don't think we had any anxious moments right the way round – it was really the most amazing ride. But the Lake needed a lot of jumping, and he was quite brilliant there. One jump into the water over a post and rails, then trot through the water and another jump in the middle. He could have found himself with too long a stride in the middle, but it didn't happen. He was perfect and we jumped out easily. He made a very, very good job of that thing in the middle of the water. I was surprised how wonderfully well he coped with such a difficult question. The idea of taking off in water and then landing in water is frightening; you don't often have to ask the horses to do it. Remember that the middle fence rises above the water – say, about a foot and a

In preparation – Lucinda Prior-Palmer lungeing Wideawake prior to the dressage test at Boekelo in October 1975.

Badminton 1976: Lucinda Prior-Palmer jumping on to the ramp into the quarry. She won the Whitbread Trophy with Wideawake only for him to collapse after the presentation.

half – but the rest is hidden, and the horse has somehow to judge the height, as well as maintain enough power to jump. If you can imagine yourself trying to run through deep water, then think of the horse trying to make an accurate take-off. It is so easy to go wrong there.

'After that, we sailed on until, towards the very end, I started getting a bit fiddly, like one does. You start to hook once too often and this is what I did at the last fence. I saw the television afterwards, and realised I had not ridden that last one well – I know I didn't – but that was not Wideawake's fault.'

After a dressage test of 40 penalties, which put them in 3rd place, Lucinda and Wideawake were very fast and clear across country, to move up and take over the lead at the end of the second day with 68.8 penalties. The horse had looked fit enough, when his turn came in the veterinary inspection, to go round the course again; and he came in to the ring for the final showjumping phase in sparkling form. Effortlessly, he jumped a clear round to confirm 1st place, and he was still full of the joys of spring after his rider received the Whitbread Trophy from HM The Queen. It was only when Lucinda and Wideawake set off on a lap of honour that tragedy struck as the horse collapsed and died; an appalling end to a partnership that had, a bare three days earlier, embarked upon a path of Olympic promise.

So, after all, there was no question as to Lucinda's choice of mount for Montreal. Be Fair, after a successful outing at Brigstock Trials, completed the team Olympic trial at Osberton and moved on to tackle what was to be his most demanding cross-country course ever – Bromont.

'Bromont?' says Lucinda. 'You needed grey matter to deal with that course; brains. Awful for us brainless riders! I don't think I've ever had to walk three times round a course and then go again because I still didn't know enough about it. It really was a very difficult test. The whole course required a lot of riding, and a very, very good horse – I fortunately had that. You had to be precise all the time, with some of those tight turns. You were always hooking back and then pushing on. One fence I was not looking forward to was the Table in the Wood, No. 8. It looked as if it was going to be awful, on that narrow, winding uphill path in the wood; but in the end it wasn't. My next worry came at No. 10, the Slalom, built on the side of the golf course. This was a treble combination of post and rails built in an open-ended square and a zig-zag down the line of the hillside.' A time-saving but perilous alternative route encompassed further hazards of trees, and the terrain out of the wood at this point was very rough indeed.

'I decided to play safe at this fence, and took the easy, long way round. I probably added an extra 12 seconds or so onto my time, but that had to be a better alternative than a certain 20 for a refusal, or worse. It could have made the difference between a place or two, but then, so could anything else, in dressage and right the way through. It was the complete turns on the steep hillside that made it so nasty; you had to brake right down to a slow speed to cope with the ground, that fell away between the different sets of rails.

'After that, the fence I next worried about was the water. I remember going into the water, Nos. 22 and 23, wondering if I was going a little bit too strong, just as one does every time when one jumps the water. But there was nothing I could do about it – either I died or I survived. It turned out that we went through there very well; but you don't know that until you land. That water, and the Badminton Lake the same year, both needed a lot of jumping. I remember them very well because one had always to take such care. You have to ride it accurately, and get the speed right – not too fast and not too slow. At Bromont, a demanding course all the way, I was very, very glad to get the water over with, because so many people had fallen there. You don't mess about when there is a jump with a take-off and landing in the water, or you end up in it yourself. Happily, I had had the advantage of jumping the Badminton one only a few months before, although I suppose the Bromont one was built first – they seem to be in the fashion.'

Lucinda and Be Fair finished the long cross-country course well clear, and the British camp heaved a deep sigh of relief to see them safely home. With the fourth fastest time of the day, the pair moved up one place to 4th, after finishing the dressage phase in 5th. It was a tough test indeed when a clear, fast cross-country round such as Be Fair's could only improve so marginally; and proved once and for all that to win at Olympic level the dressage has got to be far better than just good. In most people's view, Be Fair had performed an extremely good dressage test, but it was still not enough to shake the American supremacy.

Just as 1975 had been Lucinda's year, 1976 was not. As she turned Be Fair from the last cross-country fence to speed for home up the long run-in, she looked down at his hind legs, sensing something wrong. They passed the finish, she leapt from the saddle and even before she weighed in, Lucinda bent down to examine

Sheila Willcox jumping No. 6, the Boxed-in Rails, of the 1968 Burghley cross-country course. She won the Bass Trophy, and was short-listed for the British (Mexico) Olympic team but declined to go as reserve. She is riding Fair and Square, sire of Lucinda Prior-Palmer's Be Fair.

the off hind leg that he lifted ominously from the ground, as if in aggravation.

Within a few more seconds, he was badly lame and clearly in so much pain that it was dreadfully distressing to watch; he had to be taken back to the stables in a horse ambulance. The trouble was later diagnosed as the same that had crippled HM The Queen's grey, Columbus, when Captain Mark Phillips was poised to take a world title: the Achilles tendon had slipped off the hock.

There was no question of bringing Be Fair out for the veterinary inspection the following morning. He and Hugh Thomas's Playamar,

who had also broken down, were withdrawn, leaving only half the team to complete the showjumping phase; a disastrous end to an Olympic challenge of such bright hopes. But for Lucinda, it was a traumatic, heartbreaking, nerve-shattering climax – and the second in four months. It had been the last time she would ride Be Fair, her companion since she was 15 years old, in competition.

Lucinda Prior-Palmer, with George, is about to clear the Park Wall (fence No. 19) of the 1977 cross-country course on the way to winning the Whitbread Trophy, and her third Badminton victory. Overall, she collected 37.65 penalties, of which all bar .25 came from the dressage – the last quarter-point came from a time penalty in the showjumping ring.

He later recovered a certain amount of soundness but, at the time of writing, Lucinda finds it difficult to keep him level at faster paces. After consultations with several leading international veterinary surgeons and other riders – particularly in America – she has decided against the operation on the hock. 'Nobody could tell me of a case when it had really succeeded,' she says, 'so I thought Be Fair would stand just as good a chance, if not a better one, of coming right again if Nature was allowed to take charge. It would be fun if I could keep him happy in his retirement by taking him to a few hunter trials, perhaps, but I

shall have to get him sound first.'

The history of Be Fair, not to be found in any official Stud Book, has a somewhat rakish touch about it. He is the illicit son of Sheila Willcox's three-day-event horse, Fair and Square, who leapt the hedge one moonstruck night as a two-year-old to pay court to a retired flat-racing mare named Happy Reunion. Lucinda first went to see Be Fair when he was a five-year-old; she had answered a *Horse and Hound* advertisement offering for sale near Birmingham a chestnut thoroughbred by the well-known event horse Fair and Square, who had just won Burghley (1968) with Sheila Willcox.

'He was a real rebel,' Lucinda recalls now. 'Bolshy. He used to stand on his hind legs and refuse to jump tricky fences. Sometimes he would not leave the stable yard, and even out at exercise he would whip round and get nappy. But hunting with the Pytchley completely changed his mentality.'

No trace of his troubled past was apparent in the supremely elegant picture Lucinda made with Be Fair inside the international dressage arena of a major three-day event. The horse, obedient to his rider's direction, seemed to possess the supple grace of a ballet dancer, the muscle control of a gymnast, the suppressed power of a small jet. The presentation was set before the eyes of the spectator, rather as an actor might crave attention for the critical scene. With Lucinda in command, the audience could expect a virtuoso performance.

Hans Günther Winkler

Born in Wuppertal, Germany, on July 24th 1926, Hans Winkler is the son of a riding instructor in the cavalry. Taught to ride by his father, Hans served with the Horse Guards towards the end of World War II, and started showjumping in 1948. He made his Nations Cup début in Bilbao, Spain, in 1952 and found international fame two years later, when he won the Men's World Championship on the great Halla, a brown mare by the trotting stallion Oberst out of a half-bred mare.

In 1955, Winkler won the World Championship again, this time in Aachen, after a jump-off with Raimondo d'Inzeo. By now Halla was one of the favourites for a gold medal at the 1956 Stockholm Olympics; and despite her rider suffering a desperately painful muscle injury, the pair pulled off two classic rounds that won them the individual gold and ensured that the team gold, too, went to Germany. But Han's injury took several months to heal, which meant that he was unable to defend his world title at Aachen immediately after the Games. The title went to Raimondo d'Inzeo; in 1957, however, Winkler had his revenge by taking the European title (which replaced the World Championship) at Rotterdam on Sonnenglanz.

In her second Olympics, at Rome, 1960, Halla collected another team gold medal, but was retired to stud the following year. Hans continued to ride in successive Olympics with Fidelitas (Tokyo), Enigk (Mexico) and Torphy (Munich and Montreal), and eventually took over the captaincy of the German team from veteran Fritz Thiedemann. Hans is celebrated not only for his unrivalled collection of Olympic medals but also for his unfailing representation of the true Olympian character; patient, dedicated, able to make sacrifices and, above all, a perfectionist with his horses.

His one great dream – to breed from Halla a foal that would take her place – was destined to remain unrealized. His subsequent search for good horses led him to tragedy with the loss, in succeeding years, of two horses called Jaegermeister: one broke a bone behind the knee at Dublin and had to be put down, and the other met a similar fate on the North American showjumping circuit.

At home in Warendorf, Hans is next door to the German Olympic training centre, where he schools his young horses. He has also given much help to younger riders, notably Alwin Schockemöhle and, more recently, rising Dutch star Henk Nooren, who carried away with him from Warendorf a Winkler-trained horse, Jaegermeister III.

The thing that most people remember about Hans Günther Winkler is the number of Olympic medals he has won. At Montreal, his sixth consecutive Olympics, Hans added a silver medal to the five gold and one bronze already in his collection; and the only barrier to an attempt on another, at Moscow, would seem to be the lack of a suitable horse when the time arrives. Clearly, this is a man of determination and patience: determination to keep pace with riders half his age, and patience to conserve his good horses for honourable, rather than financial gain. His two best performers, Halla and Torphy, both jumped in two Olympic Games, and he himself has played a star role in well over 100 Nations Cups.

As a horseman, Hans is compelling to watch. A perfectionist, he schools his horses to a high standard and asks for exact obedience inside the ring. But if chance intervenes, and he has to improvise, nobody drives on with greater urgency or guts to get round the course. The man himself, however, is a complete contrast to the almost daunting impression of precision and severity he presents in competition. He speaks with humour and wisdom, not wasting words yet eminently friendly. He has faced situations of great drama during his 24 years as an international showjumper: he has struggled round an Olympic course in excruciating agony, he has stood up to opposition and prejudice from his own colleagues and selectors, he has watched his best horse undergo a life-or-death stomach operation; and through it all Hans Winkler has survived the panic and the pressure with an aura of self-control, very much his own man.

Without a doubt, the most brilliant of his horses was the little mare Halla, foaled near Darmstadt in 1944, who made her international début with Hans in 1952. The partnership electrified the showjumping circuit by winning two World Championships in the next three years and a host of other championships in Europe and North America. But it was in 1956, at the Stockholm Olympics, that Halla had her finest hour, and became, in Han's words, 'the horse of a lifetime'.

Twenty-three teams had assembled for the Grand Prix des Nations, which also comprised the individual event, and West Germany was thought to have a good chance of a medal with two such outstanding combinations as Fritz Thiedemann on Meteor and Winkler on Halla in their trio. Two other well-fancied nations were Great Britain, the champions four years earlier, and Italy, certain to be a danger with both the d'Inzeo brothers riding.

The course, built by Count Casimir Lewenhaupt, has been much discussed since that day, and by many accounts it was extremely testing. Hans describes it as 'very big and solid', and certainly the going, made treacherous by heavy rain, did nothing to help. A double of big parallels was divided by a difficult distance of 28 ft, and followed by poles over water at a related distance. The treble, always the lynch pin of any Olympic course, consisted of an oxer with a 7 ft spread followed by a gate two strides away, then another 28 ft distance to the third element, which was another oxer with a 6 ft 6 in spread. One of the treble's problems was contained at the start, when the rider had to decide whether to put in or leave out a vital half-stride before taking off for the first element; but nobody watching won any help from Halla, who stood off in the first round, put in a 'short one' in the second, and was clear over the obstacle both times.

So the scene was set for the moment that Hans recalls as 'the most memorable of my life. In the first round of the Nations Cup, I

was injured at the second last fence. I pulled a muscle very badly; I was really in pain. We were only three in the team in those days, not four, so it was really depending on three to ride, or the team would lose the chance of winning. Halla had 4 faults at the last fence, and as Fritz Thiedemann and Meteor had gone very well (for 8 faults), also Alfons Lutke-Westhues on Ala (for 16 faults), so our chances were very high. The fence that gave me the trouble was a very high and ugly vertical: it brought the horse under the fence, so Halla was catapulting from a standstill. I made a special effort not to fall off, put my knees together, and at that moment, it went bang like an arrow.'

Halla's gigantic leap had caused Hans to suffer an abdominal rupture of what is commonly called the riding muscle; and he was very soon in agonizing pain. The situation was desperate, for at half-time the West German team was in the lead with 28 faults, ahead of Britain with 32 faults and Italy with 39, and there was no spare fourth rider to help out. An advantage of only 4 faults – or one fence – over Britain was scarcely comfortable, and the British team of Peter Robeson on Scorchin' (16 faults), Pat Smythe on Flanagan (8 faults) and Wilf White on Nizefela (8 faults) were going well. Piero and Raimondo d'Inzeo had also had 8 faults apiece, and Italy only went back to 3rd place because of 23 faults from Salvatore Oppes.

As if the pressure of carrying his country's honour were not enough, Winkler's predicament was even more painful: he and Halla had taken a one-fence lead for the individual gold medal, but now looked in no state to hold off a challenge from Pierre Jonquères d'Oriola (the gold medallist four

Legends in action: Pierre-Jonquères d'Oriola at Hickstead, Sussex, challenging for the European Championship on Pomone B (1969).

years earlier), on Voulette. To those watching, it seemed certain that Germany would be forced to drop out; but Hans himself had no intention of doing so.

'I was afraid to go to hospital, in case they would not let me out. The pain was terrible; they had to lift me on to the saddle for the second round. I took some pills, but they were no good. I got stronger treatments, and I couldn't think any more, I was doped after a few moments, and had a cup of coffee to get me clear.

'But what was so nice was that the Swedish officers reduced the speed of building fences, for the second round, so as to give me more time to recover. They had a great deal of rebuilding to do, because the course was very big and very solid, and there were a lot of faults.'

Germany's second-half scores had gone promisingly. Lutke-Westhues went round for 8 faults, and Thiedemann for 4, which left them easily in command with 40 faults and well clear of the struggle for the silver medal between Britain (on 65) and Italy (on 66), separated by a 1-fault margin when the last horse from each team had still to go. Hans and Halla were last of their team to go, and spectators sat rooted to their seats as the wonderfully brave performance unfolded before them. In intense pain, Hans could do nothing to help his horse; he could only cling to the saddle round the long course, and steer Halla in the right direction.

'Just sitting as a sack, not able to do anything, and the mare carried me over Olympic fences!' Hans says. 'I was lucky in that, although Raimondo (d'Inzeo) and Merano went clear after Halla and myself in the second round, Merano had had 8 faults in the first round to Halla's 4, and there was no jump-off.' Fence after fence, Halla had taken the decisions

all by herself and leapt clear each time until finally, she was faultless at the finish to secure both the individual gold medal for Hans, and the team gold for Germany. Hans says with feeling: 'It is a wonderful memory, and a wonderful horse. The best I ever had; and the best prize I ever had was those two gold medals. My injury took a few months to heal, and so I was unable to defend my world title in Aachen shortly afterwards.'

Like several other riders of that time, Hans was initially involved in three-day events as well as showjumping, and it was in the former capacity that Halla had first come into contact with her future partner, in 1950: 'She was originally given to the Olympic committee as a three-day event horse to try. I rode her twice in three-day event competitions; we came 3rd and 4th. The mare was stationed at our Olympic International Committee headquarters, but I was not. They tried other riders with her, but they could not succeed. Then the committee decided to send her home as it seemed useless to continue, but her owner (Gustav Vierling) asked me to take her over, and I trained her for two years, before our success started at the end of 1952. After Stockholm, Halla kept going in wonderful form, and by the Rome Olympics in 1960, she was 16 years old and still the best for me. But I retired her after that.'

In 1961, Halla went to stud. Understandably, Hans' burning ambition was to breed another such as his remarkable mare, but it was not to be. 'She had eight foals altogether,' he says, 'but nothing in particular. Now she is retired; lives a quiet and nice life. She is OK at the moment, not going downhill

Laxenburg, Austria in September 1976 marked the centesimal appearance for Germany of Hans Winkler; in this Nations Cup he is on Torphy, and helped Germany into 2nd place behind Switzerland, with a 12-fault total. In his first Cup he rode Sturmwind – in Bilbao, Spain, in 1952 – for a 12-fault total.

at all. She is 31 years old, and we have made a television film in the studio together about her life.'

Since he could not breed another Halla, Hans tried to find one to buy; but, sadly, no new horse could compare with Halla. In the 1964 Tokyo Olympics there was Fidelitas, who helped to win another team gold medal; then came Fortun, who won Hans his first King George V Gold Cup in 1965; and in 1968, with the Hanoverian Enigk, he won his second King George V Cup and took part in the four-cornered jump-off at Mexico for the individual bronze medal. But the Holsteiner gelding Torphy, a compactly made chestnut with immense scope, was really the only one to follow, albeit at a somewhat discreet distance, in Halla's footsteps. It was with Torphy that Hans experienced an upsetting summer in 1972, when a row sparked off between himself and the rest of the German team on the touchy subject of Olympic training. Ultimately Hans, the team captain, whose sacrifices for the big day had long been upheld as an example to younger men, looked like being omitted from the Games on his own home ground.

Hans followed his schedule for Olympic training in his own way, but the other German riders considered the Olympic selectors were giving him preferential treatment by not compelling him to undergo the same trials as themselves. The two sides made colourful remarks on television, and by the time of the Aachen Show in early July – just eight weeks before Munich – tempers were red-hot and threats peppered the fraught atmosphere. Hans was fighting for his life; praying for a miracle to help him regain his place in the team that was to have the honour of playing host to the

A high-summer Sunday at Hickstead, Sussex, saw the masterful Winkler/Torphy combination in action during the Prince of Wales Cup competition.

Games. The pressure increased when he was left out of the Nations Cup team at Aachen, and he was all too painfully aware that there were several younger men who could have filled his place in a moment, and would do so unless he made a strong claim very quickly.

The intensity of feeling between the two camps had built up after the first two Olympic trials, one of which Hans did not attend. His absence had led to accusations about an Olympic training grant, and a potentially slanderous one of 'professional'. Thus the last day of Aachen, traditionally the gruelling Grand Prix and attended by a crowd of some 40,000, was positively his last chance. And he took it.

In supreme control as usual, Hans produced two rounds of brilliant precision from Torphy, to join Nelson Pessoa and Nagir as the only other combination with a double clear round. Had Torphy not been penalized a fraction of a fault for exceeding the time limit, Hans would have taken the Brazilian pair to a jump-off. As it was, he finished 2nd. Even more important was the reaction from the staunchly loyal crowd, many of whom were aware that their longtime favourite was in trouble. They gave Hans and Torphy a standing ovation; they cheered and applauded thunderously, and virtually acted as selectors. After that performance and that reception, the Olympic committee could hardly ignore his claim.

Outside the ring, Hans talked about the problems that had dogged him that season. He has too much integrity to pretend a confidence he clearly had not felt, and said then, candidly: 'You will have heard all about the situation from the other riders, so I don't need to go into that. But I am horribly afraid that, even after this good showing in the Grand Prix today, the selectors will leave me out. This summer has

been very difficult, but today has been terrible, with all the pressure. I have to admit I have never felt more nervous.' But Hans was wrong. The selectors did put him back into the team. Not for the Individual Grand Prix, when he had to sit watching his team-mates, but for the Grand Prix des Nations, when he won his fifth gold medal. Looking back later on those oppressive months before the Olympics, Hans recalled: 'People destroy each other when they fight – it was like a fever. We had a misunderstanding when I had a fall and could not turn up for a practice because I was in hospital. It was like stormy weather, with a big wind – like a snowball. But to my surprise, there were people who threw dirt at me as well; I received … letters. I was very glad when it was all over.'

The stout-hearted Torphy was to last another four years. But in 1975, in a sudden stable drama, Hans nearly lost him with a twisted gut. So many cases of this condition turn out to be fatal; frequently it is not possible to set up the operation in time to save the horse. But an animal of Torphy's calibre was clearly worth the try: several lengths of intestine were cut out; and by Olympic year Torphy was back in competition.

The build-up to Montreal was nothing like as oppressive for Hans as it had been before Munich. Although Torphy was out of action early in the season with a leg injury, Hans brought him back to fitness by the time of Aachen show, in May. He went on to take part successfully in the Olympic trial at Verden. But this time, the gold medal was to slip away. Torphy, jumping with all his old zest, collected only 4 faults in the first round of the Individual Grand Prix at Bromont. The second round, however, proved just a little too demanding, and 15-year-old Torphy was visibly tiring

Blinke, with Hans Winkler, competing at Lucerne in June 1974.

towards the end of the enormous course. Hans finished with 16 faults and a 20-fault overall total, to share 10th place in the Individual list with long-time friend and rival Raimondo d'Inzeo on Bellevue and the Spaniard Eduardo Amoros on Limited Edition.

A great part of Hans Winkler's reputation has been built on his quite outstanding record in Nations Cups. For over 20 years, Germany has regarded him as the reliable key man in the team; not perhaps a rider who can boast of a large number of grand prix victories, but there can be nobody who has jumped more clear rounds in Nations Cups, or who has pulled his weight so often. And this is how it was on the closing day of the Montreal Olympics in the main stadium. Jumping third for the team, Torphy's score of 12 faults in the first round was one that counted, and his single mistake at the last oxer out of the double in the second round gave a definite chance of the gold medal. What was then needed from Alwin Schockemöhle and his champion Warwick Rex was either a clear to win – unlikely on that very soft ground with tiring horses – or a 4-fault round to force a jump-off with France. But the strain on Schockemöhle and his power-house of a horse was beginning to tell. The fall of the triple bar made it a jump-off; but then the first part of the double down, at the end of the course, gave France the gold medal and Germany the silver. Hans, cutting through the pretence as usual, commented: 'I for one am very happy to have the silver medal. Torphy was simply too tired to face a jump-off; I would not have liked to ask it of him now, he has done enough.'

At the end of 1976, Torphy was officially retired, jumping in his last Nations Cup in Paris. He spends his old age at his owner's farm in Warendorf, near the Olympic training centre, as company for Halla. Hans presses on with young horses, hoping to train one special customer for future international shows. He says of the showjumping sport as a whole: 'I am so much committed to showjumping that when I give up competing, I shall be able to spend more time helping younger riders. I know that showjumping has its problems with the amateur/professional argument, but one thing is very important – that the sport continues in future Olympics.

'I like to help younger riders to train in the proper way, as I did. I was brought up as a dressage rider in the old school by my father. He was a cavalryman; sadly, he was killed in the month before the last war ended. I had always had this dream to be in the Horse Guards, just like David Niven, but when I got there, there were no horses – only bicycles! Everything was destroyed. It was war.

'After the war, I learnt a lot from Mickey Brinckmann, who combined the German dressage style with the forward seat of the cavalry, and from Dr. Rau. If you want to be that something extra, to win the championship, the medal or the grand prix, you must concentrate to do a good job. You must ask stupid questions, and spend hours, weeks, months schooling, not competing. A managing director is maybe not popular with his staff, because he must lead, not follow. Very few people have the strength and brain to do anything alone; it is not easy. I know I must go my own way, not minding about others.

'The sport is much harder now, but the art of riding has gone back from the days when the cavalry riders were schooled at places like Pinerolo (near Rome) and Saumur (France). Everything has to go so quickly now; people don't want to spend so much time making a horse or properly schooling it.'

Eduardo Amoros (Spain) on Limited Edition, during the Nations Cup, Aachen, May 1976.

People have often asked how a perfectionist like Winkler manages to keep fighting – and keep on winning against younger opposition. Hans admits: 'It has been hard to hold up the name and position I was pushed into; to take the strain of people watching so close at the exercise ring. I try to rise more above the situation, and now it is better, more sure.'

At an international show, younger riders, hoping to scrounge a few scraps of knowledge, watch his every movement like a pack of lynxes. Hans offers a telling maxim for the next generation of horsemen: 'I think today's riders must remember that to ride well they must be civilized. They need discipline and control in a game that is like tennis – full of power play.'

Frank Chapot

Frank Chapot was born on 24th February 1932 at Camden, New Jersey. The son of a salesman who rode for pleasure in his spare time and competed occasionally, Frank attended nearby Pingey School and graduated from Pennsylvania State University before military service in the USAF. Although unable to meet the strenuous eyesight test obligatory for service pilots, Chapot's ambition to fly was later realized when he obtained a private pilot's licence, for fixed-wing aircraft.

But horses were always his major interest, and early on he formed a lasting interest in racing, achieving success as an amateur steeplechase rider in point-to-points and timber races; he rode twice in the Maryland Hunt Cup. His show-jumping career blossomed through his partnership with Chado, and he joined USET in 1955. He competed at the Olympic Games at Stockholm, Rome, Tokyo, Mexico, Munich and Montreal, collecting two team silver medals and taking over the showjumping captaincy when Billy Steinkraus retired after Munich.

Chapot's arrival on USET coincided with that of Bertalan de Nemethy, the former Hungarian cavalry officer whose inspired training methods have welded together a squad of formidable strength. At the Stockholm Olympics, Chapot rode Belair; his next horse of note was the German Diamant, bought from Fritz Thiedemann. At Rome in 1960 he rode the 22-year-old veteran Trail Guide, to win a team silver medal; the next year he took the ride on one of his best-known mounts, San Lucas. The giant 17.3-hh chestnut, bred in Nevada by Interpretation out of Gold Loma, was unsuccessful racing but became a Nations Cup stalwart, establishing a record 43 starts in Nations Cups over a career lasting 11 seasons. A puissance specialist, San Lucas was at his peak in the middle 60s, taking the individual silver medal with Chapot at the 1966 European Championship in Lucerne, behind Nelson Pessoa on Gran Geste. San Lucas came closest to Olympic individual honours at Mexico when he and Frank Chapot jumped-off against David Broome on Mister Softee for the bronze medal.

Other good horses were the thoroughbred White Lightning, ridden by Mary Chapot at Mexico and Frank at Munich, the grey stallion Good Twist, and the Canadian-bred chestnut Main Spring — with whom he was equal 3rd in the world championships. At Montreal he again proved his ability to adapt with the French-bred Viscount, who had the lowest score in both the individual and team events.

In January 1965 Frank Chapot married Mary Mairs from Pasedena, California, and they have two young daughters. She had joined USET in 1962, and in 1963 became the first American rider ever to win a Games showjumping gold medal when she took the individual title at the Pan-American Games at San Paulo on Tomboy. In 1964 the partnership won the John Player Trophy for the British Grand Prix at the White City, and went on to the Tokyo Olympics. In 1968 Mary won the Queen Elizabeth II Cup at Wembley Stadium on White Lightning.

Since their marriage the Chapots have run a stud farm at Neshanic Station, New Jersey.

Once upon a time there was a small boy, who dreamt of having his own pony; his dreams came true when his sympathetic father bought a pony named Nipper who took up residence in the back yard. His young master, with an ingenious eye to money, was soon harnessing Nipper to a cart – and off the pair trotted to sell soda from the back of the cart to thirsty youngsters and their parents in the public parks. After a while, the boy and his pony went on from the parks to the big county stable, a community riding centre. And what the little boy saw there made him realize there was more to life than sitting on top of a soda cart. Other kids were riding their ponies and jumping fences; so, not to be outdone, the boy put business aside, unhitched Nipper from the cart, and taught him to jump like the rest. For hours he would watch the others, and then go and practise to see if he could do exactly what they had done. Soon, he was good enough to hold his own in competitions at the stables; eventually, his father sold the pony and bought his son a horse.

That son, Frank Chapot, became one of the best-known horsemen in the world, competed in six Olympic Games, and captained the United States showjumping team. Though Frank Chapot has come a long way since he first hitched Nipper to a soda-cart, he has not forgotten the back yard beginnings of his story. He recalls now: 'Yes, that is how I got started. I was very lucky in that the second horse my father bought me turned out to be very, very good. From then on, I was asked to ride other people's horses because of the success I had on my own; and that led on to the career I have now. The horse was Chado – I called the farm I live at after him.'

Among the numerous horses he has ridden and championships he has contested in his 20-odd years as an international horseman, Frank Chapot is typically decisive in cutting through routine events to the one moment that mattered most of all: Hickstead in 1974, scene of the Men's World Showjumping Championship. After months of preparation that included a tour of European shows, Chapot had finally been chosen to ride Main Spring, with Rodney Jenkins on Idle Dice, to represent America against tough European opposition. Chapot, 42 at the time, had been without a top-class horse; the giant 17.3-hh San Lucas had retired in 1972, and the grey mare White Lightning a year later. But the ride on Main Spring, Billy Steinkraus' Munich Olympic mount, came vacant when Billy also retired; and by July 1974 a solid partnership between two seasoned performers had been formed.

With all the excitement about David Broome, the holder; Alwin Schockemöhle, traditional rival of brilliance; Rodney Jenkins, whizzkid from the States; Paddy McMahon, European Champion; and the dashing Hugo Simon from Austria: few people gave much thought to the incredible determination and drive of Frank Chapot – until, suddenly, he had a chance to win.

'Well, I would say that probably the most thrilling thing for me was that 1974 World Championship at Hickstead. Even though I didn't do that well – I finished equal 3rd but with a foot in the water separating me from the first two. There was all the pageantry, the excitement of just getting into the top four and ride-off; and having always wanted to get in that position, that was very thrilling for me. I'd say that was the most exciting and satisfying championship of my life. I didn't win but I was certainly close to it, and walked away from being 3rd feeling a great deal of satisfaction.

'Everyone can get lucky and win one class on a big day, but the world championship was over a four-day period, very, very difficult, and that was a big thrill for me. I remember very vividly walking in the parade that Duggie (Bunn) had, and feeling emotional about it. The George V Gold Cup was the week afterwards, and it was wonderful to win, but if I had to pinpoint one thing – there it was. The feeling doesn't go off in half an hour; it takes a long time. It's a big event and everybody's looking at you. And I thought I went well enough that I was happy about it. With a little bit of luck, I could have won.

'I did think I had a good chance, but what ruined the competition was the water jump. This can so often happen, any time you ask a horse to jump water many, many times. By doing it over and over again, you'll teach him not to jump it but to jump *in* it. I hope they don't use that world championship formula again, when horses are asked to tackle water four times in a row in such a short period of time.

'It is not only the repetition. The water impresses young horses when they're green, and gets less impressive as they go on. The water is just like a dull jump after a while, if you just keep going at it over and over and over again, and very few horses will maintain respect for it. Once they touch the tape, they find that it doesn't hurt; it's not a dramatic experience so they try a bit less. Some of the best and sharpest horses have learned to be bad water-jumpers, having once been good at it – White Lightning was one of them.

'I remember very well the puissance course on the second day at Hickstead. The fences in the second round were as big as I've ever seen in my life and I can remember, on Main Spring, jumping one tremendous oxer in the centre of the field with such an effort that, when he landed, I thought he'd had a heart attack. I didn't think he could go on. It was in the one jump-off, and Main Spring tried so hard to get over it that I was certain something

had happened to him; he had either broken down or hurt himself. It took a lot out of him, that particular effort. It nearly finished him, and if he'd had to jump much more he certainly would not have made it. But as there is no time allowed in puissance, he had time to recoup, and thank God it was the next to last fence. The last one was a high wall, which he handled very well.

'But on the third day, only Hartwig Steenken and Simona went clear, and for me to have a chance, Paddy McMahon had to go bad. The last line of fences was very difficult and I think Pennwood Forge Mill really didn't handle it at all and Main Spring did. Through the three days, those courses before the final were gigantic, much bigger than anything I'd ever jumped. Very massive, very well built, very well constructed fences; but very, very high. You really had to ride, but you were at a disadvantage if you had a careful horse. Only a very bold and "scopey" horse could handle it.

'On the rest day before the final, I thought about the other three riders – Steenken, Eddie Macken and Hugo Simon. But I didn't really visualize any one being a bigger threat than the rest, because in my mind I'd ridden a lot of different horses over the years, with one thing and another; and this one ended up as a catch-riding championship. I thought I could catch ride as good as anybody and that it wouldn't be hard for me to adapt. The thing you have to remember, which everybody forgets, is that you're not getting on three bad horses. You are getting on three of the best you'll ever sit on. So it's not a question of having to get him round the course; instead, it is a horse qualified for the final and therefore better than all the rest in the

A unique pair of prestige British trophies, the King George V Gold Cup and the Queen Elizabeth II Cup, are infrequently won by husband-and-wife teams, even in different years. Here Frank Chapot receives from HM The Queen the King George V Gold Cup, which he won at the 1974 Royal International Horse Show on Main Spring.

competition bar three. It's not so tough to ride a good horse; all you need in that situation is the brakes, and to be mentally and physically prepared for the test, which I thought I was. On that final day, the fences were not big; they already had their finalists, and you don't have to have a course with height when you're going four rounds. It all ended as a very close result, with 4 faults dividing the first two after their jump-off, and Hugo and I equal 3rd by the same margin. It wasn't as if anyone had knocked up 12 or 20 faults.'

That decisive battle at Hickstead produced a real cliffhanger of a finale; it was, as the Iron Duke observed on a more momentous occasion: 'the nearest run thing you ever saw in your life, by God! I don't think it would have done if I had not been there.' It was a pity that these four were not there to spar again two years later, on the battlefield of the Montreal Olympics (Macken had turned professional, and Simona and Main Spring had retired). But the difference in format – between a world championship, protracted over several days and winding up to a quite unexpected climax – and the Olympic Games, where one round can be crucial – is a wide gulf demanding a special sort of mental preparation of a rider. Frank was well used to coping with this Olympic problem, of concentrating energy and thought into one effort lasting, perhaps, a few minutes.

'The Olympic Games are something special, of course. You go in, and out – and it's all over with, just like a quick class. But the world championships are much more exciting.'

Although he won a silver medal with the US team at Munich in 1972, pride of place in Frank's Olympic memories is given to the 1960 Games in Rome: 'It was my second Olympics

Here Mary Chapot on White Lightning at the 1968 Royal International Horse Show, Wembley, is on the way to clinching the Queen Elizabeth II Cup.

and I probably wasn't scheduled to ride at all. I didn't ride in the individual there. I took the team place of somebody who didn't do well in the Individual. I came out with the lowest score for our team in the Grand Prix des Nations and we won the silver medal. And that was with a 22-year-old horse that was de-nerved, so it was a satisfying result. They didn't name anybody reserve specifically before the Games; but at that time you only rode three people in the team event, and although I wasn't named reserve, I think I was considered so.

'It's hard to remember exactly what sort of course we jumped, but I should say that in Italy at that time the course certainly leant towards the Italians. With an Italian course designer, the Italians would probably have the edge. It would be an unconventional course with something difficult, tricky, and that's what the course was. Probably not as high as the one built for the teams at Munich in 1972 – not as thick poles – but many different problems. More distance problems, more rider problems, and height problems. At Munich, the course demanded more scope.

'Munich was also good for our team, though White Lightning, who I rode, probably shouldn't have gone. But we had nothing else. She jumped a very good round in the morning for 8 faults (the second-best score), which saved the day for the team, but she broke down in the afternoon. Billy (Steinkraus, on Main Spring) had a clear round then 4 faults but White Lightning hurt herself in the second round. She finished the course with a heavy score. She did jump again; I think she did the Fall circuit maybe one more time and then we retired her.'

A great lady, White Lightning had proved a staunch ally to the Chapots, both of whom had ridden her with considerable success in widely-varying classes. She could hardly have been more different from the colossal San

Lucas, whose deliberate and carefully-consistent performances became a byword throughout the 60s. Where White Lightning had streaked across the ring, seemingly knowing the shortcut before her rider, Chapot and San Lucas put the camera into slow-motion. With infinite patience Frank almost never attempted to push his big horse, probably forfeiting quite a few chances of 1st-place prizes. Only once did Frank ask San Lucas to beat the clock, and that was in the jump-off at Mexico for the bronze medal. As he says, the horse found something extra on that day, and came within a hair's-breadth of the bronze.

'Apart from Rome and Munich, there was Mexico, where I just missed a bronze in a jump-off with David Broome. In the jump-off I went as good as I could go — San Lucas was not a bad horse. In fact, I went, I would say, better than he could go; but Softee for sure was a faster horse against the clock. San Lucas, you know, was a puissance horse. Afterwards, I thought there was nothing I could have done any better. But, of course, along comes David and wins with a horse that was really fast. I forget what the edge was — it wasn't much, part of a second — but he did me for the bronze and I walked away from that day disappointed, because, well, it would have been nice to have the bronze. I would say the other thing about Mexico was that it was very disappointing from the team standpoint that we didn't get a medal. We had the best team in the world that year; we won every Nations Cup we went in in Europe and the States. The only place we didn't win was in Mexico. Of course, Billy's horse, Snowbound, broke down after winning the Individual gold medal and couldn't go in the team competition. The time allowed was messed up in the team event and it turned out

that if I hadn't had so many time faults we could have had the bronze. (There was, I think, only one horse that didn't have time faults and that was Softee, second round). We had the hottest team that year, in the world and yet, through the inadequacies of somebody, we didn't get a medal.

'Montreal was different. I wasn't at all disappointed for myself. A lot of people didn't give me a chance even to make the team. I had no horse except for a young horse that I'd only had jumping in the grand-prix division that year and I would say that I owe my ride on Viscount to Bert de Nemethy's confidence in me. He knew I was the only one with any Olympic experience at all, and he gave me that horse to ride. And I didn't let him down. I would say that I was unlucky in the Individual — the horse had the reputation of not being a good water-jumper and of course in the Olympic Games you jump as much water as you're ever going to jump. But I certainly don't feel I let the side down. I had the best score of our team in both the team and the Individual. I wasn't the old man that couldn't keep up with the kids, so I didn't feel too bad about it. I walked away from Montreal very satisfied.

'Of course, I would have liked to go clear in the second round of the Nations Cup on that final day; but the going was bad and nobody pulled it off. I had 4 faults. And I'd lost my glasses over about the 5th fence in that round, so I was under a bit of a handicap. They weren't smashed, and I got them back, as I pulled up, from one of the ring crew. Of course, everybody would like to win an individual medal at the Olympics; but the main thing is that you don't want to make a fool of yourself, you don't want to let down the side. You want to be competitive and be right there and have no one say: "He was the guy that

Coach Stop, with Frank Chapot aboard, in action at Lucerne in May 1976.

ruined it, that let us down." In the old days, when we used to have only three riders in the Olympic team, I can remember very vividly David Barker, the first guy to go for the English team in Rome. He had three refusals, and the team could have packed up and gone home. And what a terrible feeling that has to be, that you've ruined the whole thing. And if Bert was having me ride last, I didn't want to be the guy that really gooped it.

'There could have been that sort of situation in the jump-off for the 1976 Toronto Nations Cup: I had got two clear rounds first time, and then I was clear again with the fastest time in the jump-off – so we won. But I might have knocked everything down and not made it. That's why you've got to be creditable, to be able to say, "Look, I wasn't a disaster. I did the best I could, and it wasn't that bad." '

The biggest problem this veteran international showjumper sees ahead of him is getting the right horses: 'Even Rodney Jenkins is almost out of horses now, and I think other people have better chances of getting a horse than I do because of my age. People would rather see Buddy Brown riding their superstar than Frank Chapot. To get one going now it'll probably have to be my own horse. I've got a very good five-year-old filly out of Anakonda, by Good Twist. I don't know whether she's a Games horse – certainly not for Moscow 1980, she'll be too young – but she's a very good jumper.

'Coach Stop was a good horse but he left me after we won the Grand Prix at Lake Placid, just before the Montreal Games, and went back to his owner, who'd had two of her very best horses die. Coach Stop would have been a very strong possibility, but there's no chance of him coming back.'

Frank and his wife Mary – who joined the US team as Mary Mairs and continued to compete with considerable success after their marriage – have a stud farm at Neshanic Station in New Jersey, on land that used to be part of an Indian reservation: 'I met Mary when she made the team through our screening trials after the Rome Olympics. She was on the team the year after that, in 1962, for our European trip, and we married after the Games in Tokyo, in January 1965.'

'Horses on the farm? We stand two stallions – Good Twist and his son, Good News, who is Tomboy's foal. Good News's get are two-year-olds now, rising three, so we don't really have a good line on them yet. We have some of our own mares, as well as visiting ones. Of our own, there's probably about 15 or 16 – too many to count, with yearlings and weanlings and brood mares. Mary and I do the schooling work. We have about 50 acres, so there's plenty of paddocks. One of our mares is White Lightning, but we've never been able to get her in foal, even to Good Twist. I do quite a bit of course-building now, but I don't think there's a big thing to be made of it. You're sure not going to make a living out of course-building, if you have a family and a farm and all the horses on it to support. Listen, I'm not going to say: "I won't do anything else but course designing." I'll judge, I'll ride, I'll course design – I'll do anything as long as it's with horses.

'The future of showjumping now in America is encouraging. We're getting some acceptance from the public, a little more than we ever had before. The difficulty in America is that we have so many sports that are very, very, very popular – American football, American baseball, basketball. And there are many, many sports that people can identify with, such as tennis and golf, that they can actually see on television. Nevertheless, despite this, I would say that we are showing a little bit of improvement in sponsorship and on television. I wouldn't say the sponsorship is terrific; but it's better and going in the right direction, rather surprisingly to me. Because everybody who can pick up a tennis racket can identify with Jimmy Connors or Chrissie Evert; but who can identify with Rodney Jenkins? How many have ever touched a horse in the United States? We've been away from the horse for so long now, with using tractors and that sort of thing, that there haven't been horses on farms for years.

Neal Shapiro of the USA became known to many not only for his Grand Prix and Olympic achievements, but also for his individual mounts: Uncle Max, the ex-rodeo horse, and the superb thoroughbred, Sloopy. Here he rides Night Spree at a Royal International Horse Show, London.

'I think there is more interest now shown by television and the media. They're looking for something different so, hopefully, we're going in the right direction; although it's never going to be as good as in Europe. Still, it's something if it is going to be better than it has been here in the past.'

The standard of equestrian competition in the States and Canada is extremely high, with a bunch of gifted young riders coming up. But in the youthful US team at Montreal, veteran Chapot – old enough to be a father to the other three – proved to be top dog by a good margin. His experience and inspired determination kept the team together to within touching distance of the bronze medal.

Frank, who considers Buddy Brown the young rider to watch, knows how important determination and self-control are at top level: 'People, I think, find it exciting to watch youngsters showjumping now as the older ones drop out. But experience counts for something. Take myself at Montreal; I *had* to be that determined – after all, you only go to the Olympics once every four years. There is pressure, of course; but I think it's the way you channel the tension. Of course you're bothered by nerves; but the big thing is if it bothers you the wrong way, if it makes you feel bad, you're no good in competition. I would say that Winkler is a good example. I think that under extreme pressure Winkler is better than he is under no pressure. Whether you call it pressure or nerves, it makes people go better sometimes. Take a first-rate athlete at the Olympic Games, when the gun goes: the warm-up tactics may not have looked good enough for a gold medal; but he goes in there, they shoot the gun, and they go – and he goes better than he can at any other time, channelling those nerves in the right direction. That is the important thing – how he handles it. When you go in there and you can't come out of the box when they shoot the gun, then you should pack it in.'

A TRIBUTE TO
Hartwig Steenken

Born on 23rd July 1941 at Borwede, near Bremen in north Germany where his father farmed, Hartwig was the youngest of a large family. He rode in junior classes when 16, and in his early 20s graduated from riding school horses and attracted the notice, with the Hanoverian mare Fairness, of the German selectors. In 1965 he joined the international showjumping team, won the Men's European title in 1971 after a close tussle with Harvey Smith on Evan Jones, took a team gold at Munich in 1972, and engaged in a ferocious but successful duel with Eddie Macken for the Men's World title in 1974. His best horse, Simona, retired to stud eight months later at the age of 18.

Simona's replacement – the grey mare Erle – never fulfilled her early promise, and the very able Kosmos injured himself in a pre-Olympic trial. Luck also deserted the world champion in 1977, when Goya went off form and Hartwig had to rule himself out of the European championship. Instead, he turned professional and signed for Campari, to combat soaring costs.

It was barely three weeks after signing that Steenken, returning from a party in Hanover on Monday July 11th 1977, was critically injured when the car in which he was travelling as a passenger crashed into a bridge. The only one to be hurt, he was taken to hospital in Hanover and after a seven-hour brain operation relapsed into a long coma. He died on Tuesday 10th January 1978.

The career of Hartwig Steenken was marked both by triumph and disaster. Ferocious in his will to win, Hartwig developed a unique riding style, brilliant when it worked and wildly eccentric when it did not.

On the credit side were world and European titles, an Olympic gold medal at Munich in 1972 and a reputation that made him widely respected by his colleagues and a household name with millions of fans. On the other side of the coin were the moments every sportsman prefers to forget: missed chances at two Olympic Games brought about by human error, thus bringing the mighty 'Stinken' down to everyday level for a while. But he remained a rider always more prone to breaking the speed record than lagging behind.

As a horseman, Hartwig's approach to showjumping always appeared more natural than that of some compatriots, and he placed paramount importance on teaching a horse dressage. His approach clearly worked with the evergreen Simona, who was going great guns when she won the world title at the age of 17. But, like her master, she was wonderfully human, and a lady quite capable of changing her mind if she felt like it.

Throughout his career, the association with brilliantly able competition mares marked Hartwig as a man of sympathy and patience. He would humour and coax a recalcitrant female, understanding that a burst of temperament one day would not stop her being a matchwinner the next. He commented: 'Mares have brought me luck and success. Simona did get a bit difficult on occasions, but she was so fantastic otherwise that I just put up with it.' At Hickstead in the World championship qualifying rounds she was breathtaking in her exuberance, jumping the only double clear round over a severe Nations Cup-type course on the third day, as if tackling

a minor speed class. Hartwig, knowing she liked to be in command, sat tight and let her get on with the job. In the final, her lack of brakes was something of a problem to the other riders – Macken, Chapot and Hugo Simon – after Hartwig revved her up to 'formula one' proportions.

But it was not Simona's headstrong habits that caused disaster in January 1973. In the Munster Grand Prix Hartwig had a crashing fall from a horse called Ensor, smashing his right leg above and below the knee. It was pinned, plated and riveted, and the doctors gave him no chance of recovering to defend his European title at Hickstead that July. But they had underestimated the courage and single-mindedness of their patient. He fought back to get fit in time, and in June Mickey Brinckmann, the celebrated German course-builder, said with a happy smile: 'Hartwig? He is walking with a stick and riding like a demon!'

At the beginning of July, Fate intervened again. At the end of a knockout competition in Aachen Hartwig came through the finish hell-for-leather, swerved to avoid colliding with his opponent, and instead cannoned into the perimeter fencing. Inevitably, the newly-mended leg broke again and Hickstead was out.

A sportsman first and foremost – Hartwig's major pre-occupation outside horses was always soccer – he played a major part in a team of German showjumpers that will, perhaps, never be equalled for star quality and for friendliness. He was intensely proud of learning a little English from his opponents and, despite travelling the world, kept the direct, uncomplicated manner of the true countryman – both with his friends and his horses – and was never heard to speak ill of anyone. In an era of distinguished horsemen, he stood out as an individual of character.

The bond between man and horse has survived many centuries. But what of the future? Difficulties and controversy even now put the relationship to severe tests; professional, as well as amateur, faces problems and setbacks that would seem to have little to do with his basic desire to sit a horse. Yet there is, surely, cause for optimism.

It is not masochism that inspires a man to rise at five on a black and freezing morning to divest a row of loose boxes of their heavy load of manure. The same man, hardly recognizable in immaculate and expensive clothes, may be seen six hours later, astride his gleaming, well-fed horse, waiting for hounds to move off from the meet. Anticipation of the chase has pumped fresh vigour into his weary muscles; but by five at night, with his back aching and his eyes sore, this drooping sportsman has still the horse, his tack and his clothes to clean and the horse and himself to feed. It is a ritual that never varies.

Throughout history, men and women have braved crippling disabilities to follow hounds across country for the sheer pleasure of it. Steeplechase jockeys, some of them wired like robots to keep limbs and tendons together, set forth daily to race, often in appalling weather conditions for little financial reward. Weighed against the effort and considerable physical risk involved, the rewards of the average jump jockey are not high. But ask him if he thinks of quitting, and the answer is always the same: Never!

Nobody, it seems, could possibly be so mad as to become involved in horses in the hope of making a fortune (though dreams of winning the rich flat races must prompt the purchase of many an unsuitable yearling at the sales). Yet there *is* money to be found: in racing, and in other forms of equestrian sport – showjumping, dressage and three-day eventing. Driving and polo, which each has its own regular sponsors and followers, are growing steadily in public appeal as attractive spectator sports. (Polo, a tough, rough, fast game, would certainly have been a winner with the blood-thirsty masses 600 years ago; the Emperor Tamerlane is reputed to have played with the heads of his opponents slain in battle.)

Since the decline of the horse as a means of transport in civilian and military life, amateur and professional sportsmen have commandeered the horse. They turned him into a business; such big business that equestrian sponsorship in Britain, which has more than doubled in the last few years, soared by the end of 1977 to over £500,000 ($1,000,000) for the year.

Clearly, someone has the money to spend; but who is making it, and how? One answer is that sponsors like to back showjumping, because they get a fair return for their outlay in the press, and particularly on television; viewing figures during the two annual Wembley shows, the Royal International Horse Show and the Horse of the Year Show, are, with an estimated 10 million per night, second only to those for football. Coverage of three-day eventing, on the other hand, is much more complex: cameras have to be positioned nearly the whole way round the cross-country course to make a first-class, comprehensive and exciting programme – and this is very expensive.

It is often assumed that international showjumpers must be rich. One reads that Harvey Smith won £6,000 in a week's jumping, at the West German show of Aachen; or that David Broome amassed £5,000 in a week at the Dublin show: it sounds impressive. But offset such a win against the huge costs of running a stable of showjumpers, and it will be seen to be a mere drop in the ocean of the

178

annual budget. Horses go sick, and run up vet's bills; they go off form and win no money for months at a time; they get tired out or stale from continuous competition and have to be rested; they may cost a lot of money as promising youngsters and never make the grade; or they may simply take years of patient work before reaching a peak. They may cost a lot of money to buy, period – as the Americans say. It is interesting to survey showjumping prices since 1971, when Paul Schockemöhle sold the grey, Askan, to millionaire construction magnate Josef Kun from Homberg for £56,000 ($112,000).

Later, Cecil Williams sold Beau Supreme, the mount of Derek Ricketts, to Dutch businessman Leon Melchior for a reported £98,000; but the figure could well have been a few thousand less. In fact, the horse was bought back by Mrs. Cox for Ricketts to ride again a year later for a very great deal less money; and in 1975 had to be destroyed after breaking a leg during a competition at Wembley. The fact that Beau Supreme was not insured underlines the desperate gamble that an owner is prepared to take with his money.

The same year, 1975, saw prices still spiralling. American thoroughbred Jet Run, brilliantly promising with US professional Bernie Traurig, was bought by a Mexican millionaire for his son, Fernando Senderos, who won the individual showjumping gold medal with the horse at the Pan American Games. The price? Just under $300,000. Back in Europe, Melchior paid £110,000 to Lincolnshire farmer John Taylor for two horses successfully brought out by Malcolm Pyrah: Severn Valley and Severn Hills. The bulk of the sum concerned Severn Valley, who was taken over 12 months later (with his younger

Beau Supreme with Derek Ricketts competes in the Wembley, London, King George V Gold Cup competition, only minutes before tragedy struck.

brother, Severn Hills) by Johan Heins, and went on to win the 1977 European Championship.

Dublin Horse Show week in 1977 was a hotbed of rumours. £100,000 was reputed to be on offer for at least two horses, though not accepted; but the mind-blowing zenith was reached when Mr. Alvin Coyle of Londonderry put a price-tag of £250,000 on his 5-year-old Red Fox, competing in novice classes at the show with his son. The reason for the astronomical figure was that Mr. Coyle did not wish to sell at that particular moment; and nobody during the week called his bluff.

Income from prize money is notoriously undependable; more profit lies in the deals a rider can attract by virtue of his good horsemanship or 'eye' for a promising horse. Eddie Macken, for instance, leading money-winner in Europe in 1976, might win £20,000 – £30,000 two seasons running; but a year or two later he could be back to square one, if his best horses dropped out and he had to train a new string. Grey-whiskered veterans like Bill Roycroft, Australia's evergreen Olympian three-day-eventer, who will be 66 at the time of the Moscow Olympics (at which he happily threatens to compete) have been doing this as regularly as clockwork, for 25 years – although neither prize money nor dealing money in eventing is comparable to that in showjumping.

Going back through the annals of showjumping, to the early 1950s, one is taken aback to read so many names of today: Frank Chapot, Jim Elder, Harvey Smith, David Broome, Peter Robeson, Piero and Raimondo d'Inzeo and Hans Günther Winkler. Bill Steinkraus, America's great Olympic champion at Mexico, retired in 1973 after a long innings and now does valuable work popularizing the sport amongst millions of North Americans by his television commentaries. And Alwin Schockemöhle, Germany's champion at the Montreal Olympics, retired in 1977 but is making his

stable available to young pupils and helping to train them on. All these very experienced horsemen, who have had literally hundreds of potential showjumpers through their hands and have had to re-form their front line, as it were, many, many times, would agree on one point: only a bare handful of those hundreds have been the magic horses with the winning streak,

A July Sunday in 1971 at Hickstead, Sussex: Bill Steinkraus, much respected in Europe, demonstrates American horse-power on Fleet Apple during the Prince of Wales Cup competition. It was three years earlier that the US team captain captured the individual gold medal at the Mexico Olympics, then on Snowbound.

the ones that pay in a few days for their stablemates' oats over a year.

Europe in 1973 saw the crazy arrival of the British professional riders, all 43 of them, transformed from amateurs in an attempt to set an example of honesty before the rest of the world. Four or five years later, most of the Britons have consolidated their new status, some – Ted Edgar with Everest Double Glazing, David Broome with Harris Carpets and Marion Mould with Elizabeth Ann Kitchens – having accepted long-term patronage of a big company. Outside Britain, only a tiny group have joined the professionals.

David Broome in action on Heatwave during the Three Counties Show, Malvern, Worcestershire, in June 1975.

Nelson Pessoa, once with Pernod, is now established with Moët et Chandon. Eddie Macken and Paul Darragh both ride for the Irish tobacco firm, P. J. Carroll; but Eddie was already associated with the Irish Dairy Board through their leasing of Kerrygold. Just before his tragic accident, Hartwig Steenken became Germany's first major international rider to turn pro, when he joined Campari; Marcel Rozier put France in the picture when he relinquished amateur status in April 1977, but later said he was changing back again. American Rodney Jenkins has been a professional for over 15 years; though his decision had nothing to do with the long-rumbling controversy: turning professional was the only way he could afford to continue to work with horses.

Currently, despite the fact that he can legitimately sell more than three international competition horses per year, can openly teach pupils and be paid for it, and does not have to be secretive in accepting sponsorship help to run his stable, the professional does face disadvantages. Ted Edgar won more money as the Benson and Hedges professional champion at Cardiff in 1977 than did his wife, Liz, as amateur champion on the same day. But only Liz could earn a place in the British team for the 1980 Moscow Olympics. Had nationality permitted, however, both could have contested America's extremely valuable open Jumping Derby in September 1977 on Rhode Island, run by former event rider Mason Phelps, and worth a total purse of $76,000 (first prize roughly one-sixth of that).

The Rhode Island Derby, in fact, underlines the recent improvement in North American prize money, a situation brought about by the tax laws governing charitable

Mason Phelps with Blitz Krieg during the show-jumping phase of the 1970 Chatsworth three-day event. Seven years later he was organizing the rich Rhode Island Jumping Derby.

183

institutions. In many cases, the purses for $10,000, $15,000 or $30,000 grand prix are offered by a well-endowed charity, a healthy trend that will clearly continue to improve America's equestrian outlook.

But if regular international matches are all open, and only the Olympics remain closed to professionals, then it is surely time to hope for one of two things: an open Olympic Games, or a World Equestrian Games. Col. Sir Harry Llewellyn's firm belief, that there is a strong chance of the Olympics' opening its doors by 1984, seems over-optimistic, unless there is to be a revolution among the International Olympic Committee (IOC). Since Russia, with all her state-supported athletes, is hosting the next Games, little can be decided before 1980. After that, however, the IOC has certain facts to face: first, dedicated preparation and training are necessary to achieve Olympic standard, in equestrian events as much as in any other athletic discipline; secondly, IOC rule 26, on broken time, permits athletes to absent themselves from work and be paid by their employers with the approval of their own national federations; and thirdly, amateur rules concerning the acceptance of or making of money are flagrantly broken the world over – so much so that one is unable to name more than a very few genuine present-day examples of the equestrian 'amateur'. Such are the facts, and they speak for themselves.

Possibly more pertinent to the future of the sport is the support evinced for Col. Llewellyn's suggestion of a World Equestrian Games. He says: 'I have been asked to outline proposals for such an event. It would have to have the blessing of the FEI, who could give permission to include them in the existing calendar, midway between Olympic Games, in the same year as – but not conflicting with – the Commonwealth Games. Competitors

would be able to achieve a peak in the middle of the four-year cycle, 1982 and 1986.' This, Col. Llewellyn considers, would make things easier for selectors and trainers, and give national federations a two-year instead of a four-year outlook on the construction of first and second teams.

If equestrian events are still acceptable on the Olympic calendar by the time the Games reach 1984 and 1988, then an Equestrian Games on the alternative four-year pivot begins to sound attractive. One city would then stage a tournament with dressage, showjumping and three-day-event contests; maybe with the possibility of adding three-day-event driving and polo as well. Equestrian stadiums could be better utilised in this way, and cities could recoup some of their investment by concurrently running a 'trade fair for the horse'.

If, on the other hand, equestrian events were to be taken out of the Olympics, then an open Games for the world's horsemen could become the focal point. A country might, perhaps, in this way take her turn on the sporting scene by shouldering a small rather than a monstrously large expense. An added advantage to an open Games would be that competitors would not be expected to 'make do' on territory patently unsuited to top international competition.

Montreal provided a prime example of unsuitable territory. In the three-day event, both steeplechase and cross-country phases were built on bad ground; Bromont was, however, the chosen site outside Montreal, and that was that. The Grand Prix des Nations (team) showjumping was almost worse, if that

Bert de Nemethy, trainer of the United States showjumping team, talks to an example of the dedication to equestrian sport: Lise Hartel, winner of silver medals with Jubilee at both the Helsinki and Stockholm Olympics, where she competed (despite being a victim of poliomyelitis) in the individual dressage events.

is possible. Persistent rain had so softened the main Olympic stadium surface of grass that there was doubt about holding the last day finalé until a few hours before the start. Ironically, the fast-draining sand surface in Bromont showjumping arena, which could have seated only 30,000 of the 70,000 main stadium ticket holders, and was therefore ruled out, would have been perfect. In the end, the course for the Olympic Nations Cup, a long-awaited finalé to four years of training, had to be so far modified to make showjumping possible that it ultimately bore little relation to the master plan. The potentially dramatic climax fizzled out; a victim of inconvenient financial necessity, for Montreal could not afford to refund the expensive tickets of 40,000 pre-paid spectators.

In the years ahead, however, as in the beginning, man is linked irrevocably to the horse. Affection, the tie that binds, survives all; and surviving will continue to carry horse and rider over every pitfall, and foward into the future.

But in the meantime, as professional horsemen hurriedly pack their carpet bags and depart for the Middle East, *spare a thought for that dying race, the true amateurs.*

Richard Meade

Olympic Games

Tokyo	1964	I: 8th	T: E	Barberry
Mexico	1968	I: 4th	T: 1st	Cornishman V
Munich	1972	I: 1st	T: 1st	Laurieston
Montreal	1976	I: 4th	T: E	Jacob Jones

World Championship

Burghley	1966	I: 2nd	T: E	Barberry
Punchestown	1970	I: 2nd	T: 1st	The Poacher
Burghley	1966	I: 7th	T: 2nd	Wayfarer II

European Championship

Moscow	1965	I: 12th	T: 3rd	Barberry
Punchestown	1967	I: 20th	T: 1st	Barberry
Burghley	1971	I: 5th	T: 1st	The Poacher

Other Major Victories

Badminton 1970 (The Poacher). Boekelo (Holland) 1973 (Wayfarer II). Midland Bank National Championship, Wylye 1970 (The Poacher).

Notable Dates

1974: Awarded OBE in January for services to sport.

Horses Campaigned include

Ad Astra, Barberry, Cornishman V, Eagle Rock, Embassy, Flamingo, Goshawk, Jacob Jones, Laurieston, The Poacher, Tommy Buck, Turnstone and Wayfarer II.

Rodney Jenkins

World Championship

Hickstead	1974	I: 8th		Idle Dice

Grand Prix Victories (CSIOs)

New York 1973 (Idle Dice) and 1975 (Number One Spy), London (RIHS) 1974 (Number One Spy).

Other Major Victories include

Cleveland Grand Prix 1967 and 1977. Oak Brook Grand Prix 1967, 1969 and 1970. American Gold Cup 1972, 1973, 1974 and 1975. American Grand Prix of Florida 1973, 1974 and 1975. Los Angeles Grand Prix 1972. Jacksonville Grand Prix 1973, 1974 and 1975. American Invitational 1973 and 1977. Oxridge Grand Prix 1974. Ocala Grand Prix 1975.

Horses Campaigned include

Brendan, Gustavus, Icey Paws, Idle Dice, Nanticoke, Number One Spy and Mr. Demeanour.

Eddie Macken

World Championship

Hickstead	1974	I: 2nd		Pele

European Championship

Hickstead	1973	I: 9th		Oatfield Hills
Vienna	1977	I: 2nd	T: 7th	Kerrygold

Grand Prix Victories

St Gallen 1975 (Boomerang), Wiesbaden 1975 (Boomerang), Wembley (HOYS) 1976 (Boomerang), New York 1976 (Boomerang), Hickstead Easter 1977 (Kerrygold), La Baule 1977 (Boomerang).

Other Major Victories

Daily Mail Cup, London 1975 (Boomerang). Victor Ludorum at Horse of the Year Show 1975 (Boomerang). Professional Championship, Cardiff 1976 (Boomerang). German Jumping Derby, Hamburg 1976 (Boomerang). British Jumping Derby, Hickstead 1976 (Boomerang).

Notable Dates

1974: Turned professional after World Championship. 1976: Leading rider on North American Fall circuit. 1976: Set European record for prize money won in season – £36,000. 1977: Resumed partnership with Pele (now Kerrygold).

Horses Campaigned include

Alkazar, Boomerang, Boy, Carberry, Easter Parade, Himself, Japha, Lysander, Maxwell, Morning Light, Oatfield Hills, Pele (Kerrygold), Springtime, Weekend.

E	=	Eliminated
NC	=	No competition
N/SEL	=	Not selected
NT	=	No team
R	=	Retired
I	=	Individual
T	=	Team

HRH The Princess Anne

Olympic Games
Montreal	1976	I: 24th	T: E	Goodwill

World Championship
Burghley	1974	I: 12th	T: N/SEL	Goodwill

European Championship
Burghley	1971	I: 1st	T: N/SEL	Doublet
Kiev	1973	I: R	T: N/SEL	Goodwill
Luhmühlen	1975	I: 2nd	T: 2nd	Goodwill

Notable Dates
1967: Competed in first official BHS event at Eridge. 1971: First competed at Badminton, with Doublet, finishing 5th. 1971: Winner of Sportswriters' Award, Daily Express Sportswoman of the Year, and BBC Television Sports Personality of the Year. 1973: Married Capt. Mark Phillips.

Horses Campaigned include
Arthur of Troy, Candlewick, Columbus, Doublet, Flame Gun, Goodwill, Mardi Gras, Persian Holiday, Purple Star and Royal Ocean.

Nelson Pessoa

Olympic Games
Stockholm	1956	I: 33rd	T: 10th	Relincho
Tokyo	1964	I: 5th	T: NT	Huipil
Mexico	1968	I: 16th	T: 7th	Pass Opp
Munich	1972	I: 39th	T: NT	Nagir

World Championship
Aachen	1956	I: 7th		Relincho
Buenos Aires	1966	I: 4th		Huipil
La Baule	1970	I: 23rd		Pass Opp

Pan-American Games
Chicago	1959	I: NC	T: 2nd	Copacabana
Winnipeg	1967	I: NC	T: 1st	Gran Geste

European Championship
Aachen	1965	I: 2nd		Huipil
Lucerne	1966	I: 1st		Gran Geste
Rotterdam	1967	I: 4th		Gran Geste

Grand Prix Victories include
approximately 50 at CSIOs and CSIs throughout Europe: Aachen 1964 (Gran Geste) and 1972 (Nagir), Ostend 1966 (Caribe), and Rotterdam 1966 (Caribe).

Other Major Victories include
German Jumping Derby, Hamburg 1962 (Espartaco), 1963 (Gran Geste and Espartaco equal), 1965 (Gran Geste) and 1968 (Gran Geste). British Jumping Derby, Hickstead 1963 and 1965 (Gran Geste). Italian Jumping Derby, Milan 1967 (Huipil). Trophee Internationale, Paris 1975 (Pass Opp).

Notable Dates
1961: Moved from Brazil, firstly to Geneva, Switzerland, and then Chantilly, France. 1974: Turned professional.

Horses Campaigned include
Ali Baba, Abdullah, Camalote, Cangaceiro, Caribe, Copacabana, Corcovado, Diablito, Espartaco, Gran Geste, Houdini, Huipil, Moët et Chandon, Mr. Punch, Nagir, Oakburn, Olympia, Pass Opp, Relincho, Samurai and Saphyr.

E	=	Eliminated
NC	=	No competition
N/SEL	=	Not selected
NT	=	No team
R	=	Retired
I	=	Individual
T	=	Team

Harvey Smith

Olympic Games
Mexico	1968	I: 11th	T: E	Madison Time
Munich	1972	I: NS	T: 4th	Summertime

World Championship
La Baule	1970	I: 3rd		Mattie Brown
Hickstead	1974	I: 7th		Salvador

European Championship
Rome	1963	I: 3rd		O'Malley
Rotterdam	1967	I: 2nd		Harvester
Aachen	1971	I: 2nd		Evan Jones
Vienna	1977	I: 17th	T: 2nd	Olympic Star

Grand Prix Victories include
approximately 40 at CSIOs and CSIs throughout the world, including Dublin 1972 (Mattie Brown) and 1976 (Olympic Star), London 1972 (Summertime) and 1973 (Salvador), New York 1967 (O'Malley), Nice 1967 (O'Malley), Rotterdam 1962 (O'Malley), Rome 1963 (O'Malley), Aachen 1977 (Graffiti) and Teheran 1977 (Graffiti).

Other Major Victories include
British Jumping Derby, Hickstead 1970 and 1971 (Mattie Brown) and 1974 (Salvador). King George V Gold Cup, London 1970 (Mattie Brown). Daily Express Foxhunter Championship, London 1971 (Mannering) and 1974 (Olympic Star). Cup of Aces, Palermo 1977 (Graffiti).

Notable Dates
1958: First inclusion in British team, at Dublin. Rode leading British money winner 1963 and 1964 (O'Malley), 1965 and 1967 (Harvester), 1968 (Doncella), 1974 (Salvador). 1971: V-sign incident at Hickstead after British Jumping Derby. 1972: Turned professional after Olympic Games.

Horses Campaigned include
Archie III, Askan, Peggie's Pride (Condor, Doncella, Mattie Brown), Evan Jones, Farmer's Boy, Graf, Graffiti, Harvester, Harvest Gold, Hideaway, Johnny Walker, Lights Out, Madison Time, Mannering, Montana, Olympic Star, O'Malley, Rolling Hills, Salvador, Sea Hawk, Speak Easy, Summertime, Times Square, The Frame, Upton, Volvo and Warpaint.

Michael Matz

Olympic Games
Montreal	1967	I: N/SEL	T: 4th	Grande

Pan-American Games
Mexico City	1975	I: 3rd	T: 1st	Grande

Grand Prix Victories
Mexico City 1976 (Mighty Ruler), Nassau 1976 (Mighty Ruler), Toronto 1977 (Jet Run), and Cleveland 1972 (Rosie Report).

Other Major Victories
North American Championship, Detroit 1973.

Notable Dates
1973: First selection for USET, in Washington. 1974: Toured Europe with USET. 1977: Tour of Europe as individual.

Horses Campaigned include
Blue Line, Grande, Jet Run, Mighty Ruler, Rosie Report, Sandor and Snow Flurry.

E	=	Eliminated
NC	=	No competition
N/SEL	=	Not selected
NT	=	No team
R	=	Retired
I	=	Individual
T	=	Team

Debbie Johnsey

Olympic Games
Montreal	1976	I: 4th	T: 7th	Moxy

European Championship
Vienna	1977	I: R	T: 2nd	Moxy

Junior European Championship
Hickstead	1971	I: 11th	T: 7th	Champ V
Antwerp	1973	I: 1st	T: 5th	Speculator
Lucerne	1974	I: 18th	T: 2nd	Assam

Grand Prix Victories
Brussels 1975 (Moxy), Dortmund 1976 (Croupier).

Other Major Victories
Amateur Championship, Cardiff 1976 (Moxy). Usher's Brewery Gold Tankard, Royal Highland Show 1976 (Speculator). Radio Rentals Stakes, City of Glasgow Show 1976 (Moxy). Basildon Bond Leading Show Jumper of the Year, Wembley, London 1976 (Speculator).

Notable Dates
1975: First inclusion in senior British team, Rotterdam (August). 1976: First Nations Cup, Hickstead (April).

Horses Campaigned include
Assam, Champ V, Croupier, Moxy and Speculator.

Graham Fletcher

Olympic Games
Montreal	1976	I: 30th	T: 7th	Hideaway

Grand Prix Victories
Dublin 1971 (Buttevant Boy), Aachen 1975 (Buttevant Boy), Nancy 1976 (Tauna Dora).

Other Major Victories
Cortina Crown, Wembley, London 1970 (Buttevant Boy). Olympic Trial, British Timken Show 1971 (Buttevant Boy). Victor Ludorum, Olympia, London 1973 (Buttevant Boy). Daily Express Foxhunter Championship, London 1973 (Hold Hard). Leading Show Jumper of the Year, Wembley, London 1974 (Tauna Dora). Dunhill European Trophy, Olympia, London 1975 (Tauna Dora).

Notable Dates
1971: First inclusion in international team at Rome in May. 1976: Fractured right arm and dislocated shoulder at Hickstead during Easter meeting.

Horses Campaigned include
Brawith Park, Buttevant Boy, Clare Glen, Cool Customer, Different Class, Double Brandy, Easy Rider, Hold Hard, Talk of the North and Tauna Dora.

David Broome

Olympic Games
Rome	1960	I: 3rd	T: E	Sunsalve
Tokyo	1964	I: 21st	T: 4th	Jacopo
Mexico	1968	I: 3rd	T: 8th	Mister Softee
Munich	1972	I: 14th	T: 4th	Manhattan VI

World Championship
Venice	1960	I: 3rd	Sunsalve
La Baule	1970	I: 1st	Beethoven
Hickstead	1974	I: 5th	Sportsman

European Championship
Aachen	1961	I: 1st	Sunsalve
Rotterdam	1967	I: 1st	Mister Softee
Hickstead	1969	I: 1st	Mister Softee
Vienna	1977	I: 4th	T: 2nd	Philco

Grand Prix Victories include
Dublin 1967 and 1968 (Mister Softee), Rotterdam 1967 (Mister Softee), Leeuwarden 1975 (Sportsman), Amsterdam 1975 (Sportsman), Brussels 1976 (Philco) and London (RIHS) 1977 (Philco).

Other Major Victories include
King George V Gold Cup, London 1960 (Sunsalve), 1966 (Mister Softee), 1972 (Sportsman) and 1977 (Philco). Olympia Championship 1975 (Philco). Cup of Aces, Palermo 1976 (Philco). Professional Championship, Cardiff 1974 (Philco and Sportsman). British Jumping Derby, Hickstead 1966 (Mister Softee). Daily Express Foxhunter Championship, London 1966 (Top of the Morning).

Notable Dates
Rode leading British money winner 1959 and 1962 (Wildfire) 1961 (Discutido), 1977 (Philco). 1967: Broke leg at October Horse of the Year Show just prior to North American tour. 1970: Awarded OBE in January for services to sport. 1973: Turned professional, riding firstly for Esso Petroleum and then for Harris Carpets.

Horses Campaigned include
Abelene, Ballan Lad, Ballan Silver Knight, Ballywillwill, Beethoven, Bess, Discutido, Genoe, Grand Manan, Heatwave, Jacopo, Manhattan VI (Jaegermeister), Mister Softee, Mr. Pollard, Philco, Prospero, Sportsman, Sunsalve, Sunsherpa, Top of the Morning and Wildfire.

E	=	Eliminated
NC	=	No competition
N/SEL	=	Not selected
NT	=	No team
R	=	Retired
I	=	Individual
T	=	Team

Alwin Schockemöhle

Olympic Games

Rome	1960	I: 26th	T: 1st	Ferdl
Mexico	1968	I: 7th	T: 3rd	Donald Rex
Montreal	1976	I: 1st	T: 2nd	Warwick Rex

World Championship

La Baule	1970	I: 4th		Donald Rex

European Championship

Aachen	1961	I: 4th		Bacchus
London	1962	I: 6th		Freiherr
Rome	1963	I: 2nd		Freiherr
Aachen	1965	I: 3rd		Exact
Rotterdam	1967	I: 3rd		Donald Rex
Hickstead	1969	I: 2nd		Donald Rex
Hickstead	1973	I: 2nd		The Robber
Munich	1975	I: 1st	T: 1st	Warwick Rex

Junior European Championship

Rotterdam	1954	I: NC	T: 2nd	Fehmarn

Grand Prix Victories include

Aachen 1962 (Freiherr), 1968 (Donald Rex) and 1969 (Wimpel), Dublin 1972 (The Robber), Fontainebleau 1971 (Donald Rex), Rotterdam 1973 (Rex the Robber), London 1975 (Rex the Robber).

Other Major Victories include

Grosser Preis von Europa, Aachen 1960 (Bacchus) and 1973 (Rex the Robber). King George V Gold Cup, London 1975 (Rex the Robber). German Championship, Berlin 1961 (Freiherr), 1963 (Freiherr) and 1967 (Donald Rex). Amateur Championship, Cardiff 1974 (Rex the Robber). German Jumping Derby, Hamburg 1957 (Bacchus), 1969 (Wimpel) and 1971 (Wimpel).

Notable Dates

1957: First inclusion in senior German team at Aachen, July, when 2nd with Bacchus in Grand Prix, and winner of puissance on Marsalla. 1975: Won six classes at July Royal International Horse Show at Wembley, London. 1977: Announced retirement from competitive jumping in May.

Horses Campaigned include

Athlet, Bacchus, Dascha, Donald Rex, Dozent, Exact, Ferdl, Fehmarn, Freia, Freiherr, Kadett, Lausbub, Marsalla, Pesgo, Ramona, Rex the Robber, Warwick Rex, Weiler, Wimpel and Zukunft.

Lucinda Prior-Palmer

Olympic Games

Montreal	1976	I: R	T: E	Be Fair

World Championship

Burghley	1974	I: 10th	T: N/SEL	Be Fair

European Championship

Kiev	1973	I: 12th	T: 3rd	Be Fair
Luhmühlen	1975	I: 1st	T: 2nd	Be Fair
Burghley	1977	I: 1st	T: 1st	George

Junior European Championship

Wesel	1971	I: 11th	T: 1st	Be Fair

Other Major Victories

Badminton 1973 (Be Fair). Boekelo (Holland) 1975 (Wideawake). Badminton 1976 (Wideawake). Badminton 1977 (George) 1st and (Killaire) 3rd. Midland Bank National Championship, Cirencester 1972 (Be Fair).

Notable Dates

1975: Went to Iran in October, assisting with establishment of Pony Club. 1978: Publication of her book, 'Up, Up and Away'.

Horses Campaigned include

Be Fair, George, Killaire, Hysterical, Village Gossip and Wideawake.

E	=	Eliminated
NC	=	No competition
N/SEL	=	Not selected
NT	=	No team
R	=	Retired
I	=	Individual
T	=	Team

Hans Günther Winkler

Olympic Games

Stockholm	1956	I: 1st	T: 1st	Halla
Rome	1960	I: 5th	T: 1st	Halla
Tokyo	1964	I: 16th	T: 1st	Fidelitas
Mexico	1968	I: 5th	T: 3rd	Enigk
Munich	1972	I: N/SEL	T: 1st	Torphy
Montreal	1976	I: 10th	T: 2nd	Torphy

World Championship

Madrid	1954	I: 1st	Halla
Aachen	1955	I: 1st	Halla

European Championship

Rotterdam	1957	I: 1st	Sonnenglanz
Aachen	1958	I: 3rd	Halla
Paris	1959	I: 4th	Halla
Aachen	1961	I: 3rd	Romanus
London	1962	I: 2nd	Romanus
Hickstead	1969	I: 3rd	Enigk

Grand Prix Victories include

Aachen 1957 (Halla), Rotterdam 1957 (Halla), Ostend 1961 (Romanus), Lucerne 1962 (Romanus), Copenhagen 1962 (Romanus), New York 1970 (Terminus).

Other Major Victories include

German Championship, Berlin 1959 (Halla). German Jumping Derby, Hamburg 1955 (Halla). King George V Gold Cup, London 1965 (Fortun) and 1968 (Enigk).

Notable Dates

1952: Took part in first Nations Cup at Bilbao, Spain, riding Sturmwind. 1976: Took part in 100th Nations Cup at Laxenburg, Austria, riding Torphy.

Horses Campaigned include

Enigk, Fidelitas, Fortun, Halla, Humphrey, Blinke, Duplikat, Jägermeister, Phebus, Romanus, Sonnenglanz, Sturmwind, Terminus, Togo, Torphy and Venezuela.

Frank Chapot

Olympic Games

Stockholm	1956	I: 27th	T: 5th	Belair
Rome	1960	I: N/SEL	T: 2nd	Trail Guide
Tokyo	1964	I: 7th	T: 6th	San Lucas
Mexico	1968	I: 4th	T: 4th	San Lucas
Munich	1972	I: N/SEL	T: 2nd	White Lightn
Montreal	1976	I: 5th	T: 4th	Viscount

World Championship

La Baule	1970	I: 6th	White Lightn
Hickstead	1974	I: 3rd	Main Spring

Pan-American Games

Chicago	1959	I: N/SEL	T: 1st	Diamant
Sao Paulo	1963	I: 4th	T: 1st	San Lucas
Winnipeg	1967	I: 7th	T: 2nd	San Lucas

European Championship

Lucerne	1966	I: 2nd	Good Twist/ San Lucas

Other Major Victories include

At least 78 victories on the Fall circuit between 1956 and 1976. King George V Gold Cup, London 1974 (Main Spring).

Notable Dates

1947: Won US Junior Championship at Madison Square Garden when 15 years old. 1956: Gained first international victory, the Country Life Cup in London, riding Matador. In November, in first victorious US Nations Cup team. 1965: Married Mary Mairs, also a USET member and Olympic rider.

Horse Campaigned include

Anakonda, Belair, Chado, Coach Stop, Defense, Diamant, Good Twist, Grey Carrier, Ksar d'Esprit, Main Spring, Manon, Matador, Night Owl, Pike's Peak, Pill Box, San Lucas, Shady Lady, Sharrar, Spring Board, Tally Ho, Trail Guide, Viscount and White Lightning.

E	=	Eliminated
NC	=	No competition
N/SEL	=	Not selected
NT	=	No team
R	=	Retired
I	=	Individual
T	=	Team